THE CHRISTIAN FATHERS

The
Christian Fathers

MAURICE WILES

SCM PRESS LTD

334 01930 3
First published 1966
by Hodder and Stoughton
This edition published 1977
by SCM Press Limited
58 Bloomsbury Street, London
© Maurice Wiles 1966
Printed in Great Britain
by Fletcher & Son Ltd, Norwich

The
Christian Fathers

MAURICE WILES

SCM PRESS LTD

334 01930 3
First published 1966
by Hodder and Stoughton
This edition published 1977
by SCM Press Limited
58 Bloomsbury Street, London
© Maurice Wiles 1966
Printed in Great Britain
by Fletcher & Son Ltd, Norwich

CONTENTS

5

AUTHOR'S PREFACE

"FATHER" was an early title for a bishop. One of the bishop's main roles was to be a guardian of the true faith. So by the fourth century "the Fathers" had come to be used as a collective title for those church writers (whether bishops or not) whose writings were accepted as an authoritative source for Christian doctrine. Unlike Doctor of the Church, it was never a formal title. There was never an official list of those who qualified to be included among the church Fathers. In this book I have extended the word to include all those whose writings contributed to the clarification of Christian doctrine in the formative years up to the Council of Chalcedon in A.D. 451. I have made no attempt to say which writers deserve the honour of the name "Father" and which the obloquy of the name "heretic".

The Fathers are not well known today. The most natural way of making them better-known might have been through biographical studies of the outstanding early Fathers. Two excellent works of this kind have recently been translated into English, the two books of H. von Campenhausen, *Fathers of the Greek Church* and *Fathers of the Latin Church*. There is also available the earlier work of G. L. Prestige, *Fathers and Heretics*, the liveliest and most readable of all books in English in the whole field of early church studies. I have preferred therefore to approach the subject in this book in a different way and to give a general sketch of their teaching. The great achievement of the Fathers was the establishment of a scheme of Christian theology which in its main features has remained normative for the Church ever since. Today the value of that scheme—even

7

indeed whether it has any meaning at all— is being called more and more into question. It is important at such a time to know what that teaching was and how it was first developed. That is the task which I have tried to fulfil in this book.

Where the name of one of the Fathers appears for the first time, an approximate date is included in the text. There is also an Appendix at the end which gives a list of all the Fathers mentioned by name in the book with their more precise dates and a brief summary of information about them.

MAURICE WILES

PREFACE TO THE SECOND EDITION

THIS book was first published as part of a series with the general title of "Knowing Christianity", which declared its aim to be to "provide for thinking laymen a solid but non-technical presentation of what the Christian religion is and what it has to say in this atomic age". A book on the Christian Fathers could not perhaps be expected to contribute very directly to the final part of that objective. My primary aim was historical and expository—to describe as clearly as I could the main lines of development of early Christian thought. But my overall intention was not purely historical or expository. The beliefs that were arrived at then have remained the ground plan of almost all subsequent Christian theology; so the book was intended to provide information of importance to anyone wanting to reflect at all deeply on the nature of the Christian religion and what it has to say today. That is not the immediate subject matter of the book, but the book contains hints of how such reflection might need to go. The two concerns—historical understanding and contemporary significance—are both present, but, as one reviewer noted with relief, it is the former that is dominant. "There are signs," he wrote, "that the author is straining at the patristic leash, and perhaps we ought to be thankful that making the thought of the Fathers better-known, and not discussing its relevance for the present day, is the main theme of the book."

In the year after the book's publication I moved from a lecturership in Early Christian Doctrine to a chair of Christian Doctrine. As a result the primary concentration of my own work has shifted from purely historical studies of early doctrine to a more direct consideration of that doctrinal tradition's significance for us today. So on this book's reissue it seems appropriate to pose the question: In the light of subsequent study and reflection do I still see the significance of the Fathers for us today in the same light? Or has the patristic leash finally broken?

Sympathetic understanding and critical assessment belong together. For it is only the critic with an appreciation of what was intended, and indeed was achieved, whose criticism is likely to get to the heart of the matter. In *The Making of Christian Doctrine*, published a year after *The Christian Fathers*, I set out to assess the same area of patristic doctrine from a more critical standpoint. That study did nothing to diminish my respect for the intellectual and spiritual achievement of the Fathers. But it did reinforce my conviction that their beliefs could not be taken over as they stand to serve as ours. The reasons for that are not far to seek. The relation of any age to the thought-world of past ages is a complex business. There are always fundamental differences of outlook of which account must be taken. In this case the attitude of the Fathers to the sources of their belief, particularly Scripture, though reasonable in their own day, is one that we do not and cannot share—which is not to say that our own attitudes may not often be seriously at fault. The religious ethos of their age, with its ready assumption of the direct action of God or of his angels in the world, is vastly different from ours. The underlying philosophical assumptions with which they worked are not the same as ours either. Differences such as these run deep. Yet they do not cut us off entirely from the thought-world of the past. Up to a point we can enter into and appreciate the force of past beliefs, even when we cannot fully share them. In this book I have more than once said something like: "At this point the Fathers were seeking to give expression to a religious insight of great importance. But they formulated that insight in too precise a form. Even in their own day the precise formulation was less happy than the religious conviction it was seeking to express. Carried on into later ages it has even proved to be of serious disservice to the faith. So it may well be if we continue to affirm it in the same form today." Augustine's teaching on original sin and on the Church are notable examples of this tendency, in both its negative and positive aspects (see pp. 107–8 and 152). But what is true of Augustine's teaching on these subjects applies also over the whole field of patristic doctrine, including its trinitarian and christological constructions.

For these reasons the work of contemporary theology, to which I have attempted to contribute in *The Remaking of Christian Doctrine*, has to find its own method and its own style which is not simply a continuation of the patristic tradition. But this is not easily achieved. All theology is a strange mixture of the ephemeral and the eternal. If we eschew historical study of the Fathers because our theology is to be constructed along other lines, we are likely to fall into one of two traps. On the one hand we are in danger through lack of historical perspective of giving too absolute a status to the time-conditioned judgments of our own day. Or at the other extreme we may fall short even of that relative independence of the patristic tradition that we seek. For it has contributed through creeds and liturgy at so deep a level to the very way we pose religious and theological questions that we may find ourselves using the time-conditioned judgments of the Fathers as the criterion for assessing our own without realizing that that is what we are doing.

A study of the Fathers will not tell us directly what our faith or our theology should be. It is in the first place a historical study of great fascination. But it remains my conviction that it is also in the indirect way that I have tried to indicate an indispensable prerequisite for serious theological work in our own day.

MAURICE WILES

Chapter One

THE IMAGE OF GOD

IT is a man's image of God that counts. Automatically, and often unconsciously, it will colour every other facet of his belief. The sophisticated second-century pagan spoke scornfully of Christians as people who believed in a God in the sky, a God whose shape was the model in whose image the human body had been made. Some of the simpler Christians did think in those terms. But to the Christian scholar such people were an embarrassment. Origen, the great Alexandrian scholar of the third century, scolds them for their childish views in his sermons and firmly disassociates himself from all such ideas when meeting the protests of outsiders. The unashamedly anthropomorphic language of the Old Testament, by which God is spoken of in directly and sometimes naïvely human terms, posed a problem, but it was not an insuperable one. There is plenty of evidence in the Bible itself that such language is not intended to be taken literally. If you take the Bible as a whole seriously—and this above all the Fathers set out to do—it is clear enough that the God of whom it speaks is not a God who literally walked in the garden in the cool of the day. When the prophet challenges his hearers with the question, "To whom then will ye liken God? or what likeness will ye compare unto him?" (Isa. 40. 23), the answer he implies is that there is nothing which is adequate to the task.

But the image of God with which the Fathers worked was not drawn exclusively, or even primarily, from Scripture. Its primary source was the Graeco-Roman world to which they belonged and to which they were concerned to speak. When the Christian apologist sought to commend his faith to the pagan world he did not have to begin by convincing men of the existence of God. Indeed it was he who found himself being dubbed "atheist" because the practice of his faith dispensed with so many of the outward forms most commonly associated with religious observance. The existence of God in some sense was a conviction which he shared with all his contemporaries.

But the qualification "in some sense" is of vital importance. "God" is not a word which can be given clear and unequivocal definition. It is a flexible word, capable of bearing many diverse meanings—so many indeed that some people have been led to ask whether it has a sufficiently clear meaning to be of any value at all. St Paul speaks of the Greek world as being populated by "gods many and lords many" (1 Cor. 8. 6). In the usage of the popular religious cults of the day the word "god" was a severely debased coinage. The Christian apologist had no desire to be understood in that sense when he spoke of God. The God of whom he spoke was "God" not "god", the one true God for all the earth not one of a number of gods who were objects of worship for the varying cults of the contemporary world.

But he was not the only one who wanted to differentiate his talk of God from that which was implicit in the practice of popular worship. To some educated pagans that worship was an idle superstition which they would like to see eradicated; to others it was a proper vehicle of self-expression for the masses whose minds were incapable of following the truer way of philosophic contemplation. But all were agreed that the gods of which it spoke were not to be taken seriously. Whether the idea of them was positively harmful or whether it was a necessary accommodation to simpler minds, it was certainly not the truth. There was a

14

higher and more unitary conception of God, which was open to those who would follow the road of philosophy or contemplation.

The pioneering days of Greek philosophy were over. The founders of the great schools, Plato and Aristotle, Zeno and Chrysippus, had all been dead for more than three hundred years. The influence of their ideas continued not simply in their own particular schools but more diffusely in the general philosophic climate of the day. In thought about God, there were two main contrasting traditions—the Stoic and the Platonic.

Stoicism is a system which does not at first sight have much that would seem likely to appeal to the Christian thinker. It has no conception of the transcendent. It is moreover a materialistic system. Its highest principle— that to which it gave the name of "god"—was "spirit"; but "spirit" was not something immaterial, only a more refined form of matter, a kind of fiery vapour, immanent in all things. But this basic divine stuff was also called "Logos" or reason; it was thought of as an active immanent principle holding all things together and directing their development in a purposive harmony. This latter aspect of Stoic thought was congenial enough to the Christian; but for providing a basic understanding of the concept of God a picture which was couched so exclusively in terms of immanence, and a material form of immanence at that, could never serve. Surprisingly enough one of the most influential of the early Fathers, the North African Tertullian (c. A.D. 200), did draw upon this Stoic image of God. In overt intention he was the most violent opponent of allowing philosophy to have any influence on Christian thinking, but the loudness of his protests did nothing to avert the probably unconscious influence of Stoicism on his own ideas. He was no crude anthropomorphist picturing God as an old man in the sky, but he does seem to have

15

been unable to conceive the totally incorporeal as being fully real. St John had described God as "spirit" (John 4. 24), and so Tertullian in Stoic vein declares that "spirit" to be a uniquely refined form of corporeal substance. But the suggestion remains a curiosity without subsequent influence. It was the Platonic tradition which was to play the vital role in determining the image of God which predominates in the thought of the Fathers.

Platonism is a system which contrasts at almost every point with the Stoic. Where Stoicism is a philosophy of immanence, Platonism is a philosophy of transcendence; where Stoicism is materialistic, Platonism is spiritualistic. For the Platonist the world of ordinary things in which we live is a world of imperfection, transience and decay. But there is another world, the world of the "ideas" or "ideal forms" which is perfect, changeless and eternal. It is therefore this immaterial, transcendent world that is, in the fullest sense of the word, most real. Such reality as appertains to the things which we touch and see in this world of the senses belongs to them by virtue of the fact that they imitate or participate in the ideal forms of the eternal world. At times, in the more ethical aspects of his thought, Plato speaks of the idea of the Good as standing at the apex of the world of the ideal forms; at other times, in the more mathematical aspects, it is the idea of the One. He does not himself identify the Good or the One with God. Nevertheless they do hold in his scheme of thought a position closely analogous to that held by the idea of God in a fully theistic philosophy. The identification was a natural one not only for a Christian but for later Platonists as well.

Here then was an approach to the idea of God which was naturally attractive to the Christian thinker. The distinctive character of apologetic, as compared with other ways of commending Christian faith, is the attempt to find common ground with those whom it seeks to persuade. The

Christian apologist had material enough which he wanted to commend to the Greek world but which he knew to be strange and unpalatable to it. A revelation given to the people of the Jews, the incarnation, crucifixion and resurrection of the Son of God, a way of faith which makes "foolish the wisdom of this world" (1 Cor. 1. 20)—all this was as far as it could possibly be from providing natural points of contact with the educated Greek mind. No wonder then, if he were going to employ the approach of the apologist at all, that he was only too eager to seize upon and exploit to the full any links between his own idea of God and that to be found in the predominant and most respected of all the philosophical traditions.

The influence of Platonism

God, declares the first article of the Church of England, is "without body, parts or passions". It is not the sort of description of God that arises naturally or spontaneously from the Bible taken by itself. It comes straight from this Platonic tradition which the Fathers shared with the most thoughtful of their pagan contemporaries.

"Without body"—this was the simplest and most basic way of disassociating one's idea of God from all crudely anthropomorphic pictures of him. There was no real conflict or difficulty here for the man who aspired to be both philosopher and student of the Bible. The simpler Christian who believed that Moses really did see God's hinder parts was at fault in not recognising the metaphorical or allegorical intention of the scriptural writings. Prophets and New Testament writers alike had insisted that God does not dwell in temples made with hands. When Jesus spoke of him as "our father which art in heaven", he is not to be understood to be speaking in a local sense. If God were literally "in" heaven, then heaven would be greater than the God whom it contained. God is transcendent not in the

17

lesser sense of being above or beyond this physical world of ours; he is transcendent in the more absolute sense of being altogether separate from material existence of any kind.

"Without parts"—this idea is closely linked with that of being without body. Bodies are subject to corruption and decay. The process of corruption is the process of the body's dissolution into its component parts. The incorruptible nature of a being without body derives from its not being made up of parts into which it is liable to be dissolved.

The concept of unity is one that has an enormous fascination both for the philosophic and the religious mind. In the Platonic tradition the ideal form of unity, the idea of the One, which has so supreme a role in the world of the ideas, is a unity without parts, a unity without differentiation or division of any kind. It is a unity of this absolute kind that Christians claimed to be characteristic of the God whom they affirmed. "God is simple, uncompounded being," says Irenaeus of Lyons (c. A.D. 180); "no parts are to be ascribed to God; for the One is indivisible," says Clement of Alexandria (c. A.D. 200); "God is one and altogether simple," says Origen.

The Bible also speaks in emphatic terms of God as one. But the concern of the biblical tradition is to declare the falsity of all forms of polytheism and idol-worship. It is the fact that there is only one and not many Gods that is there taught. This is not necessarily the same thing as to say that God is one in the sense of being a simple undifferentiated unity. The Fathers thought themselves to be doing no more than giving full and worthy expression to the biblical teaching about the divine unity. In fact they were doing something more than that. They were developing that teaching in terms of a particular conception of unity. That conception, the idea of a simple undifferentiated unity, is a mathematical ideal. The development was natural enough; it happened unconsciously without deliberate intent. But its implications for Christian doctrine are enormous. The idea of one who is in a full sense Son of God sharing the divine nature is a difficult enough idea to work out and to express in terms of Jewish monotheistic faith. But once transform the biblical conception of the one God into the Platonic concept of God as a simple undifferentiated unity, and the already existing difficulty is raised to the level of logical impossibility.

"Without body", "without parts" and "without passions". To say that God is without body is to exclude only the cruder forms of anthropomorphism. Man is more than a mere body; he is at least body and soul. And the shortcomings and frustrations of human life are not limited to its bodily or physical aspects. They apply also to the psychological realm, to the realm of man's emotional life. The Christian looked forward to a liberation not only from all those ills the flesh is heir to but also from all the changeableness and instability of man's moral and emotional life. In speaking therefore of God and of the divine nature it was just as important to insist that God was free of this second form of human limitation as it was to insist that he was free of all purely physical limitation. It was necessary to point out that it was not only the cruder physical imagery of the Old Testament which required a metaphorical manner of interpretation; the less obviously crude language ascribing emotional attitudes to God is also anthropomorphic in character and must be understood in the same kind of way. The Bible, says Origen, is being just as metaphorical when it speaks of the wrath of God as when it speaks of him as arising out of sleep.

The idea of the wrath of God is admittedly a special case, raising peculiar problems of its own. But the insistence that God is without passions is concerned with something more basic than the appropriateness or otherwise of the use of the particular term "wrath" with relation to God. It was concerned with the way in which any psychological term can be applied to God. God, says Clement, is impassible, without anger, without desire. Men become angry or feel desire as a result of an awareness of some lack in themselves or through the impact of external forces upon them. But God neither lacks anything in himself nor is he influenced from without as we are. All that God is and does is conditioned by his own will, by the nature of his own all-sufficient being—not by what comes to him from outside in the form of human actions or even human needs. To deny this seemed to make God in some sense at least dependent on his own creation, to destroy the proper recognition of his transcendence. To describe God as "without passions" was not intended to depict him as totally unconcerned about the world like the gods of the Epicureans; it was intended rather to stress his complete moral self-sufficiency, to show that his ways are determined not by external happening but solely by what he is. Nevertheless it was an emphasis which posed serious problems for the Christian apologist. For if this view of God's nature be taken seriously, it becomes almost as difficult to speak convincingly of the love as of the wrath of God. Can a God who in his very nature is "without passions" be also a God who sends his Son to heal the sins and miseries of the world? And can that Son be divine in the same understanding of the word while carrying out that work of healing by means of the suffering and death of the cross?

Thus the idea of God as "without passions" stands in close relation to the idea of God as "without body". The God who is altogether above the human limitations of physical existence is equally above the human limitations of psychological existence. But the idea of God as "without passions" stands in a similarly close relation to the idea of him as "without parts". Human passions are changing things; they represent the fluctuating character of human experience. But such variations cannot be postulated of a God who is simple, uncompounded being. That which is perfect cannot change; for if the change be for the better it argues imperfection in the past, if for the worse imperfection in the future.

Here again biblical language could be quoted in support of such ideas. The Bible speaks of a God who is ever the same and who does not change as men change. But as in the case of the divine unity, the Fathers were giving to the words a more developed sense than that which they bear in their original biblical usage. Where the biblical writers were affirming the reliability and consistency of God in his attitudes of grace and of judgment towards men, the Fathers were interpreting them of a metaphysical change-lessness of a very different character. And this latter sense of the word is one that cannot without grave difficulty be affirmed of the God of the Bible. Can a God who is change-less as the Platonic ideas are changeless have become incarnate at a particular moment in human history? Can indeed even an act of creation be affirmed of such a God?

Certainly it was no naïve or childish image of God with which the Fathers worked. It might have simplified their task if they had regarded the language of the Bible as giving literal descriptive accounts of God and of his ways of acting in the world. But they never made that mistake. Their mistake, if mistake it be, lay rather in the other direction, in their tendency to equate the living, creator God of the Bible with the changeless, passionless perfection of the absolute of Greek philosophical thought. Instead of the positive imagery of a God who is active and purposive love, they tend to define God by the kind of negative category which we have been considering. God is without body, parts or passions. That list of negative attributes could be greatly increased. The process is carried through to its logical conclusion, until we find God spoken of as inconceivable and ineffable, beyond thought and beyond words. Such a description is not just the language of unconsidered hyperbole. The point is made on logical grounds. The mind grasps things and names them by a process of classification. But that which is unique, and not only unique but simple uncompounded being also, cannot be classified. It follows logically therefore that if God be worthily understood he cannot properly be comprehended or described.

Such an admission might be expected to be the death of theology. What point could there be in attempting to comprehend that which cannot be comprehended and to describe that which cannot be described? "Whereof one cannot speak," wrote Wittgenstein at the end of the *Tractatus*, "thereof one must be silent." It sounds sensible enough advice. But too easily and too often it can be taken to mean whereof one cannot speak with precision, one must keep silent. And then it spells the death of a good deal more than of theology. When the Fathers spoke of the ineffability of God, they were not doing themselves out of a job. Indeed it tends to be the most voluminous of the early writers who most stress the divine ineffability. The fact that we are unable to comprehend or to define properly the divine nature does not mean that we cannot say some things which may be of help towards an understanding of God's character. There are times when our eyes cannot bear to look directly at the sun itself; they have then to infer its existence from the rays of light which reach us. So, though we are incapable of conceiving or describing the being of God himself, we can know him from his works, which stem from him like the rays from the sun. Such a view of the ineffability of God will not preclude theology altogether. It leads rather to a healthy recognition of the indirectness and the incompleteness which must always characterise every form of theological endeavour.

But the idea of the logical inaccessibility of God to the

normal processes of human reasoning carried with it a further suggestion, and one still more congenial to the Christian mind. Once human reason has acknowledged its own inability to reach up to God, it may be the more ready to accept that God has chosen to disclose himself. The hiddenness of God makes the idea of revelation the more necessary. The man who would know the unknown God can know him, says Clement, only by divine grace and by the Logos which proceeds from him.

Chapter Two

THE DIVINE CHRIST

The divine Logos

The heart of Christian faith is the person of Christ and what God has done in him. The thoughtful Christian might find himself in substantial agreement with the cultured pagan in his definition of God's changeless nature and eternal being. But that was not all the Christian apologist wanted to convey to the pagan world. He wanted to convey the heart of his faith, the meaning of Christ and of his work. And he wanted to do so in a way that was consistent with those underlying convictions about the nature of God which he and many of his pagan hearers held in common. How without simply abandoning the idea of God's eternal changelessness could he describe the divine action in creation and in history? How without doing despite to the idea of the divine unity could he speak about a Son of God in addition to the Father? How without appearing to align himself with the crudest of the old fables about the Greek gods could he talk about the birth of that Son into the world? These were the problems which pressed in upon the earliest Fathers, not only in the execution of their apologetic task but also as they tried to give expression to the faith in a way which was satisfying to their own minds and consciences.

The problem is one that poses itself at once to any sensitive reader of the Bible. It impinged with particular intensity upon those who read their Bibles in the light of the Greek philosophic tradition. It was appropriate therefore that the first attempt by Christian thinkers to give a reasoned answer to the problem should have been one which made use of a concept drawn from that same source. "The man who would know the unknown God can know him only by divine grace and by the 'Logos' which proceeds from him." "Logos" was a term with a long and respectable philosophical ancestry, and at the same time it was one which seemed well suited to give careful expression to the ideas implicit in the Christian account of divine revelation.

It is a word which is notoriously difficult to translate. Its normal English renderings are "word" or "reason". To us those sound like two distinct, alternative meanings. But we ought not to look upon them in that light; we need rather to think of them as two aspects of a single idea. Reason is always potential word and words are expressive of reason. It is not difficult to see that, while we distinguish them with two different terms, the two ideas of "the word which gives expression to the reason" and "the reason which gives meaning to the word" could be covered by the single term, "Logos."

Its role as a philosophical term goes back to one of the earliest of the Greek philosophers, Heraclitus. But it was in Stoic thought that it had come to play a role of major importance. There, as we have already seen, the word was used to describe that inherent principle of rationality which the Stoic believed to be the underlying reality in the universe as a whole, the thing which made the world go round. This was the highest reality of all in the Stoic system and Stoics therefore spoke of it as divine, as god. But the philosophy of the day was eclectic, and before the rise of Christianity the term was already being adapted for use in very different schemes of thought. It was being put to use also in Platonic systems, which unlike Stoicism believed in a transcendent realm of ideas, and in theistic systems, which

25

believed in a transcendent God. Here it could still convey the idea of an inherent rationality in the world as a whole, but it could fulfil a further function at the same time; it could help to provide a much needed link between the transcendent reality of the spiritual world and the world of ordinary sense experience. For the Platonist rationality is an essential feature of the world of the ideal forms; for the theist reason could readily be identified with the reason of God. Logos was a term that was readily at home in both worlds; it had a natural place in the transcendent divine realm as well as in the world of men. The fourth evangelist, with this background in mind, together with that of the "word of God" which came to the prophets of the Old Testament, had already taken the step of using it to introduce his record of the life and work of Jesus. No term could have seemed better suited to the task which lay to the hand of the second-century Christian writer.

How without simply abandoning the idea of God's eternal changelessness could he describe the divine action in creation and in history? How could God be a self-contained being and yet without suffering change or loss reach out to a created world? If this was a problem which the Christian felt with an especial acuteness because he was the more firmly convinced of the vital nature of God's reaching out to a created world, it was still in substance a problem which was felt in some measure by any theistic philosopher of his age. If they shared a problem, they could also share a solution to that problem. "It is patently evident," says Tertullian, "that your philosophers regard the Logos as the creator of the universe." So then would the Christian. As a word going out from the mind of a man does not deprive the speaker of the meaning which it expresses, no more need the outgoing activity of the Logos of God in creation affect in any way the changelessness of God and his inherent Logos. In the double sense of the term Logos was the answer

26

to the problem of how God could be both a changeless self-contained being and at the same time be an active creator God.

The same answer that served for the more general question of creation could serve also for the more specifically Christian question of God's self-revelation. The language in which the Old Testament spoke about God's coming down to the earth and speaking with men might clearly be metaphorical. But it was equally clearly a metaphor of something, and there were difficulties about ascribing even that something to God himself. Those difficulties were not so acute if it was the Logos which was in question. "It was not the Father of all, who is not seen by the world, 'who comprehendeth the earth with his hand and with his span the heaven', it was not *he*," writes Irenaeus, "who came and stood in a very small space and spoke with Abraham, but the Logos of God, who was ever with mankind and taught men the things of God." It was the Logos of God and not the Father who was so active in the affairs of men in the era of the Old Testament revelation, just as it was the Logos of God and not the Father who in the fullness of time was made flesh in the person of Jesus Christ.

Did such ideas involve a desertion of monotheism? Justin Martyr (c. A.D. 155) speaks incautiously of the Logos as "a second god". But if challenged for his indiscretion, he has his lines of retreat well prepared. His defence is grounded in the double sense of the word "Logos". When one speaks, as one does have to speak, of God and his Logos as distinct from one another, one should remember that it is of God and his expressed Logos, his outgoing word, that one is speaking. And that Logos is also the inherent Logos, the internal Reason of God. They are not two different Logoi; the only difference is a difference of condition. God was never without his Reason and so the inherent Logos has always been with God and can be no more separated from him than a man's reason can be separated from the man himself. When the Logos goes out from God for the work of creation and revelation, there is no question of a new being coming into existence; it is the same Logos in a new guise. Nor is there any question of any detraction from the being of God. The outgoing of his Word does not denude him of his Reason; one torch can be kindled from another without diminishing the first.

There was yet another way in which the concept of the Logos seemed singularly well adapted to the needs of the Christian apologist. The "scandal of particularity" was widely felt then as now. To the non-Christian it seemed arbitrary and irrational to claim such absolute importance for the particular historical person of Jesus. Men who lived before his time or who never heard his name have shown evident signs of goodness and of sanctity. Is it reasonable to assert that Jesus is the sole and necessary source of man's salvation? The Stoic who spoke of the universal cosmic Logos or Reason inherent in the world as a whole spoke of it also as present in germinal form in the rationality of individual men and women. Reason in each of us exists there by virtue of our participation in the universal Reason. But if it be that same universal Reason which was incarnate in Jesus then all men are unconsciously responding to him in so far as they respond to the light of that Reason which is in them by nature. "Christ," says Justin, "is the Logos of whom every race of man are partakers, and those who, like Socrates, have lived in accordance with that Logos are Christians, even though they may have been regarded as atheists."

To view Christ as the Logos of God appeared therefore to offer a most fruitful approach for the thought of the Christian theologian. Monotheistic faith and new experience of Christ; Greek ideas of the divine transcendence and biblical ideas of the divine activity; the belief that even

28

Gentiles "shew the work of the law written in their hearts" (Rom. 2. 15) and the belief that "there is no other name under heaven given among men, whereby we must be saved" (Acts 4. 12)—to all these convictions the Christian theologian was anxious to do justice. The concept of the Logos seemed to enable him to do just that. Yet for all that it was not along such lines that the key to the future of Christian theology lay. Logos was not to be the dominant concept in terms of which the Church was to define its understanding of the person of Christ and of his relation to the Father.

The Fathers were the scholars of the Church, and both halves of the definition are important. They were scholars, seeking to express the faith in as intelligent and coherent a form as they could devise. But they were not working in a vacuum, nor in the setting of a modern secular institution. They were scholars of the Church, continually in touch with the day-to-day worshipping life of the Church. The use of the Logos concept largely grew out of the needs of the apologist. Apologetic was a part of the Church's task. But it was not the Church's most basic and most characteristic activity. More fundamental was public worship and private devotion. For the ordinary Christian, Christ was the Saviour God, the object of his worship, his praises and his love. It was hardly natural in such a context to think or speak of Christ as Logos. Logos was a scholar's term; it was not well fitted to meet the religious needs of ordinary folk. St John, who uses the idea of the Logos in the prologue to his gospel, goes on in the main body of the text to speak of him as Son. It is as Son with his Father that he shared the divine glory before the world was (John 17. 5); it is as Lord and God that Thomas acclaims him as he kneels in adoration at his feet (John 20. 28). This is the language of religious devotion. The inherent Reason of God, or even the expressed Word of God, was a pale substitute. The religious consciousness of the Church saw in Christ an eternal divine being. It was not easily to be convinced that divine Logos was an adequate term to serve as the fundamental description of the divine nature of the Lord whom it loved and worshipped.

All this might not have been decisive if the Logos concept had shown itself to be eminently valuable as an intellectual and apologetic tool. But here also, even in its own natural sphere, its value proved to be less than might at first have been anticipated. The solutions which it appeared to offer to the intellectual puzzles of the early Christian thinkers turned out to be illusory. Take by way of illustration the problem of people visited by God in the stories of the Old Testament. God, the Father of all, could not, it was argued, have come down to speak with Abraham, for the divine nature is incapable of movement or of being contained in a space. Yet the story was emphatically the story of a divine revelation. But if the story be understood of the divine Logos, it was claimed, no derogation would be done to the divine nature of the Father, and since the Logos is one with God, the inherent Reason which is inseparable from him, the revelation would still be in the fullest sense a divine revelation. But clearly this solution is no solution, and it was not long before its weakness was felt. For either the Logos is of the same divine nature as the Father, in which case the objections which held in the case of the Father hold in the case of the Logos also; or else the Logos is not of the same divine nature, in which case the works of creation, revelation and incarnation are not in the fullest sense works of God himself. The Logos theologians had tried to have it both ways and it could not be done. If the truly divine is incompatible with the world of change and of matter, then no middle term can bring the two together. The problem had been posed in terms which made any answer an impossibility. In so far as the concept of the Logos was thought to have achieved that impossible task, it was a false answer to a false problem.

The attempt to frame a theology of the divine Christ in terms of the Logos of God was a failure, but it was a noble failure. It was never fiercely repudiated, nor totally abandoned; but it did gradually lose the centre of the stage. Theology underwent a gradual change of emphasis rather than a sudden reversal of direction. Many of the ideas which it had suggested lived on in new settings. Some of those which were eventually lost were lost to the detriment of the Church's thought and life. The idea of a link between the universal Logos incarnate in Christ and the fragmentary Logos present in every man provides a dimension to Christian theology which has often been unhappily absent. But, be that as it may, it was clear by the close of the second century that the primary terms in which a Christian theology of God was to be worked out were the terms "Father" and "Son". These were far more central to the biblical revelation; they were far more central to the worshipping life of the Church. But they didn't simplify the task of the Church's theologians.

Father and Son: Two Attempted Short Cuts

God the Father and God the Son—was it not the end of monotheism even to pose the question in such terms? Was not the only conceivable solution to the problem a repudiation of some part of the basic evidence? We hear of two groups at Rome about the end of the second century whose ideas, if accepted, would have removed at one stroke the central difficulty with which the early Christian thinker was faced. We hear of them only at second-hand, for none of their own writings have survived. They represent obvious ways out of the dilemma which the Church had to face; the Church recognised them as such and rejected them unhesitatingly and decisively.

31

Need Son of God imply divinity? The first group, initiated by Theodotus the leather-worker from Byzantium, denied the divinity of Jesus. They were critically-minded scholarly men of a rationalist turn of mind. Jesus, they taught, was a man—virgin-born, uniquely endowed with divine power at his baptism, a miracle-worker (what is a problem to the rationalist of one generation is not necessarily a problem to the rationalist of another)—but not different in kind from other men. We can't be sure of the details of Theodotus' teaching. We can only be sure that in denying the divinity of Jesus (in whatever way precisely he did that) he was in complete conflict with the main religious tradition of the Church. No solution along such lines had the remotest prospect of winning the allegiance of the Church as a whole.

The other group, usually called Sabellians after their chief proponent Sabellius from Libya, stood at the other end of the spectrum of possible belief. Need God the Son imply any distinction from God the Father? Need they be more than differing names for differing aspects of God's self-revelation? There was no threat here to monotheism; for there was only one God, operating now in his capacity as Father, appearing at other times in his capacity as Son. Nor was there a threat to the worshipping life of the Church, for what higher or more worshipful role could be ascribed to Christ than to identify him with God himself? For that reason it was a more attractive, a more tempting solution than the other. None the less it was rejected with almost equal speed and equal decisiveness. The biblical tradition spoke of a Son who shared the Father's glory before the world was. What sense could be given to such language if Father and Son were no more than differing aspects of the one God's self-revelation to mankind? Such a solution rode roughshod over too much of the biblical evidence. And at the same time it trampled still more

32

harshly on the susceptibilities of the philosophic mind. The unity of God with which the sensitive scholar was concerned was no mere numerical unity; it was a unity of absolute simplicity and changelessness. Such minds had no place for a chameleon-like God who could turn himself from Father into Son and back again. All that the Logos idea had fought so determinedly, even if unsuccessfully, to safeguard concerning the changeless being of God was thrown away by this theory without even a struggle. If there be no real distinction between the Father and the Son, then it was God himself, the transcendent Father of all, who suffered on the cross. Away with such blasphemy! Or, as the difficulty has been put in more modern times, if there be no distinction of persons in the godhead and Christ be the incarnation of God himself in his totality, who was sustaining the world as God lay in the cradle at Bethlehem?

Origen

God the Father, God the Son—the distinction between the two was not to be denied. But how then was monotheistic faith to be preserved? This was the problem that faced the Church of the third century and it was a problem that could not be shirked. The thought of the third century is dominated by the figure of one man, Origen. He was the most many-sided of all the early Christian writers. He was apologist and preacher, biblical exegete and philosophical theologian. He shared to the full the spirit of those whose thinking was grounded in the developed Platonism of the contemporary world. For him the God who was one was "one and simple", one with all the overtones of the mathematical philosopher's ideal. But he shared also to the full the religious spirit of those whose faith was grounded in devotion to the person of Jesus. In his interpretation of the Song of Songs as an allegory of

33

Christ and the human soul he gave to that devotion a form and an expression which was to nourish it for many centuries to come. So he felt in his own person the tensions of his age, and he had moreover the restless, inquiring type of mind which must look for their resolution not in some one-sided truncation of the truth but rather in an all-inclusive synthesis which would do justice to all the apparently conflicting aspects of the evidence. If anyone was equipped for the task, he was the man. But was the task one which could be done at all?

Origen found the framework for his attempted solution to the problem in the philosophical outlook of second-century Platonism. Two persistent problems had helped to determine the direction in which later Platonism had developed. In the first place there was the urge to try to give a more satisfactory account of the relation between the transcendent realm and the physical world than that which is suggested by the writings of Plato himself. In addition there was the desire to distinguish more firmly between unity and multiplicity within the transcendent realm. The outcome of these two pressures was the growth of a conception of the transcendent or divine realm as existing in three ranks. At the top was the one, the supreme existent, the truly transcendent. It may also be called the good, but strictly nothing can be said of it; it is ineffable and incomprehensible. Yet emanating from it in such a way as to leave it unimpaired and unaffected in its utter transcendence is the divine mind; as mind it contains within itself the various ideas or ideal forms of the Platonic scheme. And thirdly there is the world-soul, emanating from the divine mind and mediating between it and the world of sensible experience. A scheme of this kind is most clearly exemplified by the writings of Plotinus, the Neo-platonist philosopher, who was a younger contemporary of Origen. Plotinus indeed speaks of that which is divine as existing in three "hypostases", three entities. It is unlikely that he or Origen knew each other's work at first hand. It is certain, however, that they were both well versed in the work of the same second-century Platonist philosophers. Both are building in different ways on the same ground plan.

To Origen this ground plan must have appeared heaven-sent. The most naturally congenial of the non-Christian philosophical traditions had been led to the conclusion that the divine must exist in three "hypostases". Christian tradition spoke quite independently of three divine beings, the three "hypostases" of Father, Son and Holy Spirit. Where philosophy provided the form, revelation could supply the content. Moreover, in respect of the first two "hypostases" (ideas of the Holy Spirit were very little developed at this stage) there seemed to be a very good fit between the approach of the philosophical and the Christian traditions. At the top was the Father, the supreme God; to him could be ascribed with naturalness and propriety all the highest philosophical intimations of transcendent unity. Had not Jesus himself prayed to his Father that men "might know thee, the only true God, and Jesus Christ whom thou hast sent" (John 17. 3)? The Father then was the one true God of philosophical reflection and religious aspiration.

In Scripture the Son is given many titles. He is the wisdom and the righteousness of God; he is the truth and the life. Like the divine mind of the Platonic scheme, he embodies in himself all those ideas or attributes which find their expression in the good things of human life. If the Father is unity absolute, the Son is a unity capable of comprising in himself all those various goods to which human experience testifies. And because he is in himself all these various things, he can adapt himself to meet the varied needs of men and to suit their varying capacities.

35

He is the exact image of the Father; in him the perfect simplicity of the Father's being is refracted into the varied attributes of divinity; in him therefore is to be found divinity accessible to men. All this moreover is an eternal relationship. God was never without his wisdom or his righteousness; nor did he suddenly decide to express his being in some new way. Such an idea would be totally incompatible with the idea of his eternal changelessness. The divine must always have existed in two (or three) "hypostases". If we are to speak, as it is natural to do, of the Father "begetting" the Son then that "begetting is as eternal and everlasting as the brilliance produced from the sun".

But for all its intellectual breadth, for all its religious feeling (and the brief account given here does scant justice to either), it was not a solution which the Church was able to adopt. It was a genuine and profound attempt in terms of the best thought of the day to show how Father and Son could be distinct and at the same time so linked within a common divinity that the oneness of the essential godhead would not be undermined. But from the standpoint of the Church's religious consciousness the scheme still suffered from the same fatal defect as the work of the earlier Logos theologians, with whose ideas it has so much in common. The divine unity is preserved by firmly subordinating the Son to the Father; he is "god" and not "the god", as Origen puts it; "god" and not "God", as we may more freely translate him. The declaration of Jesus that "my Father is greater than I" (John 14. 28) is true, says Origen, in every respect of the Son's being in relation to the Father. Even the insistence on the Son's eternal generation from the Father is not the exception that at first it seems. The same argument about the changelessness of God that led Origen to assert the eternal existence of the Son led him also to assert the eternal existence of all rational beings.

Every human soul has existed eternally, deriving its existence from the Father through the Son. Eternity in Origen's scheme does not belong exclusively to the divine "hypostases"; it is a characteristic of all created beings also.

Despite the spirit of personal devotion to Jesus which shines through so much of his preaching, Origen insists that strictly speaking prayer can be offered only to the Father. When we offer our prayers to the Son, what we are really doing is asking him to convey them to the Father, the supreme God, the ultimate recipient of all true prayer. But in the long run the verdict of the Church was clear. Praying to Christ was not to be explained away in this manner. It was not enough to dub him "god" in some secondary sense. The Christian trinity was not to be identified with the three-tier hierarchical trinity of Neoplatonic speculation. This was the issue which came to a head decisively in the early years of the fourth century in the conflict over the person of Arius.

Arius

Origen's attempted solution of the problem how to ascribe a place to the divine Christ within the godhead which would be consistent with monotheism had involved giving to the Son a secondary status; it had meant placing him in a lower rank below the supreme Father. This seemed the most obvious line of approach to the question and had in one way or another been followed by all the early theologians of the Church with the exception of the Sabellians. If the mind of the Church had clearly been uneasy about all such attempts, it had not yet been articulated in any explicit or final repudiation of such an approach.

Arius stood within that same broad tradition. Indeed he explicitly claimed to be doing no more than affirm the faith of his forefathers. It is a common claim in religious con-

37

troversy but need be none the less sincere for that. The starting-point of his thought, he declared, was acknowledgment of the "one God, alone unbegotten, alone everlasting, alone unbegun, alone true, alone having immortality, alone wise, alone good, alone sovereign". It was the old starting-point of the philosophical tradition in Christian thought. To that extent his claim to be a traditionalist is justified. From such a strongly held version of that old standpoint neither the changeable God of Sabellius nor even the second eternally begotten divine being of Origen's system was an acceptable idea. I have argued that Origen's idea of the Son's eternal generation did not really rescue his system from its essentially "subordinationist" character, but it had certainly done a good deal to mitigate its impact. The idea of the Son deriving his being eternally from the Father and reflecting his essential attributes was a concept of rich religious value, which did much to counteract the fact that Origen had given to the Son a distinctively and decisively secondary status within the godhead. But for the rigidly logical mind of Arius all idea of an eternal generation had to be firmly excluded. It was inconsistent with the initial acknowledgment of the "one God . . . alone everlasting".

Origen had drawn a firm line between the Father who was the only true God and the Son who was god in a secondary sense, but the edges of the line are somewhat blurred by his insistence on the eternal generation of the Son and the Son's perfect reflection of the Father's attributes. Origen had also drawn a firm line between the Son and the created realm, but that line also is somewhat blurred by the fact that for him all rational beings were co-eternal with the Son, the divine Logos or Reason from whom both their being and their rationality derived. Arius had the sort of mind which didn't like blurred edges. The first line in particular must be drawn with complete

38

firmness and clarity so that the absolute unity and transcendence of the Father might be fully safeguarded. The secondariness of the Son's divinity must be more effectively underlined. The way which Arius found to do this was to insist that, though they were both admittedly to be called divine, there was a difference between them at the most fundamental level of being; to use the Greek word which Arius used, there was a difference of "ousia" or essential being between them. Only so could the proper transcendence of the Father be maintained. The Father alone was properly called God, was God in his own right; when the Son was called God it was a courtesy title, not something that was his in his own right but something that he derived at second-hand from his Father.

If you make one line of double thickness, the one next to it is likely to appear thinner even when objectively it may have been left unaltered. Arius had no desire to blur the second line between the Son and the rest of the creation. But in practice it often seems less firm than it was intended to be, because of the extreme vigour with which the first line between the Father and the Son is drawn. The Son was not eternal, for there could not be two eternals. Must one therefore say that he was temporal, brought into being at some specific point in time? Arius had no wish to say that and tried to steer a middle course. He was not eternal but nor was his coming into being a temporal event. It was necessary to say that "there was when he was not" to guard against the false view of his co-eternity with the Father; but it would be misleading to say that "there was time when he was not" for his being is prior to all notions of time. In the same way, he was not to be spoken of as a part of the Father or an emanation from him, for all such ideas would destroy the perfection of the divine unity and blur the essential distinction of "ousia" between the Father and the Son. Yet to call him a created being without further qualification would be equally misleading in the opposite direction. So Arius describes him as "a creature but not as any other of the creatures". St Paul had called him "the firstborn of every creature" (Col. 1. 15). Was not this most naturally understood as setting him within the created realm, yet apart from all the rest of the creation in a totally unique relationship to the supreme Father of all? Such was the rank that Arius sought to give to him. And in doing so he believed himself to have tradition, reason and Scripture on his side.

Arius drew his picture with a firm hand. The difficulties stand out in the paradoxical language which at places he was forced to employ. But more importantly still the main contours of the picture stand out with unmistakable clarity. The Church could see what was involved if you tried to solve the problem of the godhead by subordinating the Son to the Father and then went on to work out the consequences with relentless logic. The Church as a whole was clear enough that it did not like what it saw. A majority in the Eastern Church were inclined to believe at first that all that was wrong was the relentlessness of the logic. Arius had gone too far; but if one stopped a little earlier on the road, if one got out before the terminus, all would still be well. Athanasius was convinced from the outset that the issue was more radical than that. It was not a matter of refurbishing the picture by thinning down a line here or there. It was the whole approach that was at fault. The picture needed to be drawn in a totally different style. Slowly but decisively the whole Church came in the end to see the problem through his eyes.

Athanasius and the Council of Nicaea

To Athanasius, Arianism was not a misleading interpretation of Christianity; it was not Christianity at all. It could be Judaism with its solitary God; it could be Greek philosophy with its "unbegotten" replacing the Father God of the Bible; it could be Greek polytheism with its gods of different rank. The one thing it could not be was Christianity. Every Christian was baptised "in the name of the Father and of the Son and of the Holy Ghost"; was that one name a conjunction of beings of different orders of existence? Christian worship was offered to that same Trinity and prayer was regularly made to the Son; were Christians then guilty of worshipping a being of the created realm? Most important of all Christ was the Christian's Saviour. Only a truly divine saviour could save; only one who was divine absolutely and in his own right could impart to man a share in his own divine nature, make them "partakers of the divine nature" (2 Pet. 1. 4) which was the essence of their salvation. Arianism spelt doom to all the religious values of Christianity; it was the death of the Christian religion. No true progress could be made unless it were absolutely and unequivocally rejected.

The outbreak of the Arian controversy coincided with the early years of Constantine's reign. This provided a situation in which concerted action by the Church as a whole was both desired by the monarch in the interests of the unity of the Empire and practically facilitated by the new standing of the Church in relation to the authorities of the state. So the coinciding needs of Church and Emperor led to the meeting of the Council of Nicaea in Bithynia in A.D. 325, a gathering of 318 bishops, almost all of whom came from the Eastern church. Large gatherings of bishops are not occasions of theological construction. The Council did what it could be expected to do. It repudiated the teaching of Arius. Even the apparently positive statements of the formula which it promulgated are primarily negative in intention. The Council's creed is not the Nicene creed familiar to many from the worshipping life of the Church today. Our "Nicene creed" was in fact the creed of a later Council at Constantinople in A.D. 381. But the two most crucial phrases are common to both creeds. The Son is "of one substance", in Greek "homoousios", with the Father. Arius had underlined the essential distinction between the Father and the Son by insisting that it was a difference at the most fundamental level of being, a difference of "ousia". The only way to refute such teaching without possibility of mistake or evasion was by using the same terms which he had used. Father and Son are not distinct in "ousia"; they are of the same "ousia", or "substance" as the word has come to be translated in this context. What all this meant is best illustrated by a second phrase from the creed, "very God of (or 'from') very God". The words translated "very God" are the same as those which are translated "true God" in the high-priestly prayer of Jesus to the Father that men "might know thee, the only true God and Jesus Christ whom thou hast sent" (John 17 3). Despite the conclusions which Origen, and still more forcefully Arius, had drawn from that text, it is illegitimate to distinguish between the Father and the Son as between true God and god, God in the fullest sense and god in a secondary sense. The Son is "true God from true God". If he derives from the Father, he is none the less God in the same full and unqualified sense that the Father is God.

But all that does nothing to solve the problem of how the Christian is to understand the nature of the godhead. It is to restate the problem in a way which excludes the Arian approach. The problem remains. There is the Father and the Son; both are God in the same full meaning of the word; but there is only one God. The divinity of the Son is not to be squared with the unity of God by making him god in a lesser sense. The whole attack upon the problem by means of ascribing an inferior status to the Son is to be ruled out altogether. All that was implied by saying that the Son was "of one substance" with the Father. But it does nothing to show how the two are one God. If it were to suggest any answer to that question at all, it would be the old Sabellian answer. Father and Son are then after all different facets of one being or substance. The suspicion that it might imply some such idea was the reason for its only receiving very reluctant acceptance into the vocabulary of the Church's thinkers. It did come in time to be fully accepted, but only gradually as it proved to be an indispensable bulwark against Arian ideas. But the problem was still there. How could Father and Son be distinct and yet one God?

The Cappadocians and the doctrine of the Trinity

The final phase in determining the main structure of that Christian doctrine of the godhead which has remained the common conviction of the whole Church ever since was the work of the second half of the fourth century. Half a century had passed since the days of Nicaea. They had been hard times for Arianism's most vigorous opponents. Athanasius was exiled five times from Alexandria before his death in A.D. 373. But by the end of that time the tide had turned. Nicaea's rejection of Arianism had received broad and general acceptance in the Church at large. The foundations were now firm. The time for construction had come. The chief architects were three close friends; two brothers, Basil of Caesarea, leader and statesman, and Gregory of Nyssa, scholar and mystic, together with their friend Gregory of Nazianzus, orator and poet. The three together are usually known, after their home area in Asia Minor, as the Cappadocian Fathers. It is to them that we owe the first clear sketch of what was to become the orthodox trinitarian doctrine.

Their first task was to establish that it was a trinitarian

43

doctrine that was needed and not just an account of the relation of Father and Son within the godhead. The existence of the Holy Spirit as in some way within the Christian godhead had never been denied, but it had largely been neglected. As long as thought about the second person of the Trinity was primarily expressed in terms of the divine Logos, it was natural to associate all forms of the divine activity of an immanent nature with the Logos; those who thought in such terms did not deny the reality of the Spirit, but they felt little need to develop thought about his role within the godhead. As long as Arianism centred its attack upon the difference of "ousia" between the Father and the Son, it was there that the main concentration of the Church's thought also was directed. But by the second half of the fourth century these conditions no longer obtained. Christians had always spoken of Father, Son and Holy Spirit. It was natural that in course of time men should begin to concern themselves not only with the relationship of the Father and the Son but with the role of the Spirit also. When they did so the same arguments that had played so decisive a role in Athanasius' opposition to Arianism came again to the fore, and were brought to bear upon the new question. Like the Son, the Spirit also figured in the doxologies of Christian worship and the formulary of Christian baptism. If Father and Son were of the same fundamental order of being, identical in "ousia", was it reasonable to suggest that the third member of the triad was not to be classed with them in fundamentally the same way? If the Son must be fully divine to fulfil his saving function, the same must be true also of the Holy Spirit; for his work of sanctification was nothing other than the implementation in human life of the Son's saving work, making men to be partakers of the divine nature. What was true of the Son had to be true of the Spirit also. If the idea of a descending hierarchy within the godhead were ruled out as a blasphemous absurdity in the case of the Father and the Son, it could hardly be brought back in again in the case of the Holy Spirit. If the Son was "homoousios" with the Father, so must the Spirit be also. The creed of Nicaea had done no more than affirm belief in the Holy Spirit; the creed of Constantinople (our Nicene creed of A.D. 381) goes on to describe him as "the Lord, the life-giver, who with the Father and the Son together is worshipped and glorified". Probably in deference to the less explicit nature of the scriptural evidence in the case of the Holy Spirit, it does not directly describe the Spirit, like the Son, as "homoousios" with the Father. None the less that is what it meant, and that is what it was taken to mean.

All this the Cappadocians had to establish. They weren't simply arguing with a long dead Arius. They had living and lively opponents to be overcome—latter-day Arians, like Eunomius, a man of powerful logical acumen, or the so-called "spirit-fighters", like Eustathius of Sebaste, who resisted the new developments of thought about the Holy Spirit. Nevertheless the feel of their position was very different from that of Athanasius. Athanasius had needed not only to refute the teaching of Arius but to convince the main body of the Church that Arius' whole approach was fundamentally mistaken. The Cappadocians had a firmer base from which to operate. They still had to argue, but their opponents were further out towards the fringes of the Church's life. Thanks to the labours of Athanasius, the roots of their thinking were more securely grounded in the soil of the Church's self-consciousness than his had been. The things for which Athanasius had fought, even the consolidations of that position which they themselves had won, were broadly accepted in the thought of the Church. They were not simply the conclusions of an argument, they were agreed foundations of all further thinking. The

Cappadocians *knew* that Father, Son and Holy Spirit were all fully God, each "homoousios" with the other and, despite a few hesitations about the Spirit, the Church as a whole knew it with them; Arianism was a spent force. Similarly they *knew* that Father, Son and Holy Spirit were distinct entities; Sabellianism had been vigorously denounced in the third century and had died a second death in the earlier years of the fourth, when attempts to understand the Son's identity of being with the Father in such terms were uncompromisingly rejected. On the basic facts of the case, the Church's mind was clear. She was free to resume in a new spirit of confidence her attempts to explain how the facts could be such as she was convinced they actually were.

Father, Son and Holy Spirit were one. They were one in fundamental being or substance, one in "ousia". The term had been used at Nicaea and had won full acceptance as the appropriate term to describe the unity of the godhead. But Father, Son and Holy Spirit were also three, and there was no agreed correlative term to describe their distinctness from one another. The term "hypostasis" had been used in that context by Origen, but it had also been used freely as an equivalent to the term "ousia". Basil insisted that the two terms must be distinguished. Father, Son and Holy Spirit were one in "ousia" and three in "hypostasis". The adoption of a new term can be a useful aid to discussion; it cannot by itself solve anything. It is the meaning of the terms that matters.

We speak of Father, Son and Holy Spirit as three persons. Gregory of Nyssa uses the illustration that the word "persons" in its ordinary meaning suggests to us. Peter, James and John are three people, but they share a single human nature. So, it might seem, the Cappadocians were really tritheists after all; Father, Son and Holy Ghost are three gods, sharing in a single divine nature. That is how it seemed to some of their contemporaries; that is how it has seemed to many of their interpreters ever since. Nevertheless it is a false seeming. The treatise in which Gregory discusses the example of Peter, James and John is entitled "That we should not think of saying that there are three Gods". Gregory was a thorough-going Platonist. For the Platonist the universal is more real than the particular. Strictly speaking, says Gregory, we should not speak of three men, but of three participants in the one, unique "idea of man", the single, real "humanity". So the divine "ousia", which is common to the three persons of the godhead, is not some abstract, conceptual notion of divinity which each has separately; it is the one, unique reality of God. It is admittedly difficult at first not to read Gregory in tritheistic terms; but so to read him is to misread him.

As we read on, beyond the basic illustration, the monotheistic intention becomes clearer. The different persons are never to be thought of in separation from one another. None ever acts apart from the others. We ought not to think of a Father who made us, a Son who redeemed us and a Holy Spirit who sanctifies us, for every act of God is an act of the whole and undivided Trinity. So after a time it may come to seem that far from being tritheists they are really unitarians or Sabellians denying the reality of the distinctions between the three persons. Like many another thinker since, the Cappadocians rejoiced in the fact that they were attacked from both sides. They saw in it confirmation that the path they were following was the right one. The Christian view was the mean between Judaism and Hellenism; between monotheism on the one hand and popular polytheism on the other. If they were accused of under-emphasising the unity of God and also of destroying the distinctness of the persons, it was a sure sign that they had found the true *via media*. The charge that they had

47

done away with the distinctions between the persons they vigorously repudiated. It was only separateness in their activity that they denied. The conjoint nature of the activity of the three was the necessary evidence of their unity of being. But it did not do away with all difference between them. It only meant that those differences were not reflected in the divine activity in the world. They belonged exclusively to the realm of inner relations, the interrelation of the three persons to one another. The distinguishing mark of the Father, as the name suggests, is his being the unbegotten source; the distinguishing mark of the Son, with equal obviousness, is his being begotten, his generation from the Father; the distinguishing mark of the Spirit was less self-evident—the definition that ultimately found most favour was one drawn from St John's gospel (15. 26) which speaks of his procession from the Father. In earlier systems, like that of Origen, similar ideas had played their part in descriptions of the Trinity as a descending hierarchy of beings. But now they were all contained as distinctions within the one coequal reality of God. What meaning was to be attached to them in such a context? This the Cappadocians do not venture to declare. For all the boldness of their speculations they had a very profound sense of the mysteriousness of the divine being. That such distinctions exist, we could know, they claimed, in the light of the divine revelation. What the distinctions really constitute it was not given to us to know. They belong after all not to the realm of our experience, the realm of the divine activity, for there the whole Trinity always acts conjointly. They belong to the realm of the divine being itself, a realm which we should never forget is strictly ineffable and incomprehensible to mankind.

Augustine and the Athanasian Creed
With the Cappadocians the main lines of development

48

are at an end. Later thinkers touch up the picture here and there; they do not alter the main structure. We have traced that development almost exclusively in terms of the Greek-speaking churches of the East. The West was less given to speculative thought. It could live less uneasily with the paradox of the three and the one, without continually struggling to find some intellectually cogent resolution of the paradox. At a very early stage, by the close of the second century, Tertullian was speaking of one "substance" and three "persons" of the godhead. The detailed outworking of his views bears the marks of that "subordinationist" approach which was characteristic of the early centuries. But such marks were in a form that could be allowed to drop away quite easily without agonising reappraisal or violent debate. The main outlines of his theology, even the precise language which he coined, could without too much straining become the vehicle for expressing the same essential doctrine as that elaborated so painfully by the Cappadocians in the East.

But at the close of the period, a generation after the Cappadocians, when the real struggle was over, there arose in the West a thinker unrivalled by any other figure in the whole story of the early Church, save that of Origen. Augustine's (c. A.D. 410) doctrine of the Trinity is the same as that of the Cappadocians, but he sees it from a different perspective. It is not possible for the human mind to hold its view of the three and the one in equal focus. One can give them equal value on the written page, but the mind needs to make its approach from one side or the other. The East (with the important exception of Athanasius) tends to approach from the side of the three, the West from the side of the one. When an Easterner spoke of God he thought most naturally of the Father, with whom the Son and the Spirit must somehow be joined in one coequal godhead. When a Westerner spoke of God he thought most naturally

49

of the one triune God, within whose being real distinctions of person must somehow be admitted. Thus while the Cappadocians could use, with careful qualification, the illustration of three men, it is not an illustration that could commend itself to Augustine. If the word "person" were to be used in the normal human sense of God at all, declares Augustine, it would have to be used of the one rather than the three. The use of the word to refer to the three must not be understood in such a sense. The distinctions between the three, as the Cappadocians had said, were a matter only of their relations to one another. If the word "person" were understood in its literal sense, it would be grossly misleading. Augustine continues to use it, he says, only because it has become traditional and he knows of no alternative but silence.

How then from his perspective could Augustine illuminate the mystery of the triune God? What illustration could he employ that would not prove more misleading than helpful? The Cappadocians had balanced on occasion their illustration of three men with the long established illustration of an individual man and his Logos. It was this second type of illustration from individual human life which Augustine chooses to develop. Did not Scripture say that God had created man in his own image? In man therefore (man, that is, before the separate creation of woman) we may look not merely for an illustration but for an actual image of the triune God. Augustine pursues his search for this image of God in man with all the subtlety of psychological insight which was the most outstanding feature of his intellectual greatness. The threefold character of the life of man upon which his attention was mainly centred was man as consisting of memory, understanding and love. Just as it is essential to interpret the Cappadocian illustration of the three men from the standpoint of their Platonism and not from that of our empiricism, so it is essential to interpret Augustine's image from the standpoint of his psychology and not of ours. These different faculties in man had for him a measure of real distinction from one another; they were more than just attributes or properties of the mind. On the other hand they were not separate entities either; they were no more parts of the mind than they were its attributes. They were overlapping and interlocking realities, distinct yet inseparably inherent in each other. Moreover, each faculty corresponded with a peculiar appropriateness to those characteristics which Scripture and tradition associated with the several persons of the Trinity. For the Platonist, the soul of man is immaterial and unlike the body belongs properly to the true world of the ideas; knowledge of that ideal world is made possible when the soul, reminded by objects in the world, remembers the forms of the ideal world which is its own original and true home. It is therefore memory which is the ultimate source of any knowledge of the truly real. Memory is therefore an appropriate image of the Father. "Reason" and "wisdom" had a long history of association with the person of the Son. So wisdom or understanding arises out of the memory, out of the source of man's knowing, in a way that is analogous to the Son's generation from the Father. Love also, the first of the fruits of the Spirit, had a similarly long history of special association with the person of the Holy Spirit. It is moreover the conative element in human experience; as the desire to know binds together the source of knowledge and the cognitive faculty of knowing and leads to the actual effective realisation of knowledge in the life of man, so, says Augustine, the Spirit "suggests to us that mutual charity whereby the Father and the Son love one another".

Augustine never claims that his images are other than very faint and very incomplete. After all the image of God in man has been defaced, even though not destroyed, by

51

human sin. That faintness and that incompleteness can, however, in Augustine's view, be mitigated in part as we allow the defaced image in ourselves to be "renewed after the image of him who created" us (Col. 3. 10). In other words, any further progress in understanding the being of God must be by a process that is as much devotional as purely rational. That claim should not be regarded as an attempted escape from the challenge of clear thinking. Rather it is a reminder that the spirit of detachment, important though it is to critical thought, may at times prove a barrier to the deepest insights. Augustine's work, even more than that of the Cappadocians, was aimed not so much at proof as at a fuller exploration of what he believed to be already known.

Without such exploration, in which thought is mingled with devotion, what is known remains a bare structure. The culmination of the Fathers' agreed convictions finds classic expression in the so-called Athanasian creed, which is neither by Athanasius nor a creed. Its author is unknown but it seems to have been composed in southern Gaul during the fifth century as a useful compendium of instruction.

"This is the Catholic faith, that we worship one God in Trinity and Trinity in unity, without either confusing the persons or dividing the substance. For the Father's person is one, the Son's another, the Holy Spirit's another; but the Godhead of the Father, the Son and the Holy Spirit is one, their glory is equal, their majesty co-eternal . . . The Father is God, the Son God, the Holy Spirit God and yet there are not three Gods but one God . . . The Father is from none, not made nor created, nor begotten. The Son is from the Father alone, not made nor created but begotten. The Holy Spirit is from the Father and the Son, not made nor created nor begotten but proceeding. And in this Trinity there is nothing before or after, nothing greater or less, but all three persons are co-eternal with each other and coequal."

An assessment

What are we to say of this doctrine? How are we to assess the achievement of the Fathers? The Athanasian creed is not an attractive work. It is easy to criticise, but it is particularly easy to criticise for the wrong reasons. It is easy to treat it as something it was never intended to be, such as a positive affirmation of the faith suitable for singing on special festivals, and then criticise it for failing to fulfil the role for which we have miscast it. If we take it for what it is, a formal outline summary of the Fathers' thought about what must be true about the godhead in the light of the divine revelation in Christ, then three main lines of assessment lie open to us. We can say that the Church was wrong to insist on the full divinity of Christ and that therefore the whole complex development of trinitarian doctrine was an unnecessary and misguided construction. To say that, now as then, is the thing that more decisively than any other has been understood to set a man outside the Christian fellowship. We can say that it does embody in outline form the structure that all thought about God must follow if it is to remain true to what is implicit in the records of the New Testament. The Fathers would not want us to say more, and would wish us, like Augustine, to find our own ways in thought and devotion to breathe life into the bare bones of its formal outline. If we are reluctant to give either of these answers, there is a third course that we can follow. We can call into question the basic image of God, the underlying Platonist framework in terms of which the Fathers sought to elucidate their thinking. We may believe that within those terms of reference they have given the best possible answers, but question whether those terms of reference are the only ones or, for us, the right ones. We may claim that the task which they undertook in their way must be undertaken today in some new and very different way. But if we do say that, we should not underestimate the size of the task which we are offering to undertake. Its magnitude will be no less than was theirs.

Chapter Three

THE INCARNATION

The inescapable fact

"In those books of the Platonists," wrote Augustine, "I found, not indeed in the same words but to the self-same effect, enforced by many and various reasons, that 'in the beginning was the Word, and the Word was with God and the Word was God. All things were made by him; and without him was not anything made' . . . But that 'the Word was made flesh and dwelt among us'—this I found nowhere there" (*Confessions* 7, 13–14). Augustine exaggerates his point, but the point itself is valid. The developed Christian conception of the divine nature had much in common with Neoplatonist ideas. Even the difficult notion of a threefold differentiation within the godhead, though not to be found in precisely the same form in Neoplatonism, had its close parallel there. But the idea of the Word made flesh was not only absent from the writings of Platonism; it was in direct contradiction of its most fundamental convictions. The basic premiss of the Platonist approach was the absolute distinction between the eternal world of the ideal forms and the unstable world of physical phenomena. Within such a scheme of thought it was hard enough to envisage God as creator and as active within the empirical world; but for the divine Word to become flesh was not just difficult to conceive, it was unthinkable. Yet it was just this that the Christian Church was committed to proclaim.

The first step was for the Church to make it clear beyond mistake that it was an incarnation, and nothing less, which she was committed to proclaim. We have already seen that those who, like Theodotus the leather-worker, regarded Christ as a specially endowed man, virgin-born and miracle-worker, but in no full sense divine, never even began to win over the main body of the Church to their view. There was a greater appeal in the claims of those who called into question the true humanity of Christ. St John's first epistle (4. 3) tells us of the existence already in New Testament times of some who denied "that Jesus Christ is come in the flesh". Christ was a divine saviour; that was the fundamental conviction of the majority of ordinary Christians. But a divine saviour could not, it was argued, have sullied himself by actually becoming flesh. Any incarnation therefore must of necessity have been a matter of appearance rather than reality. A divine Christ could not have gone through the degrading experiences of human birth; the birth stories should be excised from the gospel records. A divine Christ could not have had a body subject to the normal processes of nourishment, digestion and evacuation; his eating and drinking must have been a matter of appearance only. Above all a divine Christ could not have undergone the agonies of death on the cross; it must have been Simon of Cyrene who was crucified in his place.

The expedients which were required to square the gospel narratives with the conception of an exclusively divine Christ were too drastic to be plausible. The striking thing is that the attempt should have been made as vigorously and as variously as it was in the second century. It is a measure of the difference of ethos between the age of the Fathers and our own.

Those who were prepared neither to dissolve the historical tradition in this way in order to suit their own convenience nor yet to accept the offensive notion of an incarnation of the divine sought a less violent solution. Justice must be done to the human and the divine elements. There was a human Jesus and a divine Christ, but the two were always necessarily separate and distinct beings. One did not have to deny the birth narratives in order to avoid the blasphemy of saying that the divine was born; it was the human Jesus who was born. The divine Christ-spirit was associated with him only from the time of his baptism, from the day on which God said, "Thou art my beloved Son; this day have I begotten thee" (Luke 3. 22: alternative reading). One did not have to postulate a substitution of Simon of Cyrene as the man hanging on the cross in order to avoid the blasphemy of saying that the divine was crucified; it was the human Jesus who died. The divine Christ was no longer with him then, as he showed when he cried, "My divine part, my divine part why hast thou forsaken me?" Such an approach does a little less violence to the historical tradition, but only a little. The central figure of the gospel story and of the Church's faith was a single figure, Jesus Christ, and not two distinct beings, a human Jesus and a divine Christ. Irenaeus declares that when St John brings his gospel to a close by saying that "these things are written that ye might believe that Jesus is the Christ, the Son of God" (John 20. 21), he had foreseen those blasphemous systems which would divide the Lord into two separate beings, "Jesus" and "Christ", and was determined to forestall them in advance by insisting that Jesus and the Christ were one and the same being. He was wrong about the intention of St John's words, but his point stands.

When Irenaeus and Tertullian, who says the same kind of thing still more forcefully, denounced all such attempted explanations of Christ's person as utterly incompatible with true Christianity, they were not simply acting in defence of historical realism. They were doing that. They did see themselves as witnessing to a reliable historical tradition, while their opponents indulged in fanciful myth-making. But they saw their insistence on the real humanity of the divine Christ as having vital religious significance as

57

well. Christ must have been divine to be saviour. That fact was not in dispute. But nor was it all that needed to be said. It was through the fault of a man, says Irenaeus, through the disobedience of the first Adam that sin had established its hold upon human life. For that hold to be undone the same agency was required; it could only be rightly achieved by the obedience of a second Adam, who was as fully man as the first had been. For the divine Word to make us sharers in the divine nature, he must have reached right down to us by sharing in ours. "He became what we are that he might bring us to be what he himself is." In similar vein Tertullian insists that Christ must have become wholly man if the whole man is to be saved. Man is not just a spirit but flesh and spirit. If the Word did not become flesh, then flesh has been left outside the sphere of redemption. The possibility of full salvation depends on the reality of the incarnation.

So it was nothing less than incarnation that the Church was committed to proclaim. The facts of the historical record and the requirements of the message of salvation alike demanded it. It was Tertullian who, with characteristic clarity of mind, first sets out in systematic form the essential outline of the Church's conviction. Christ had a truly divine and a truly human nature, or, to use Tertullian's word, he was made up of two "substances", divine and human; but these two were combined in a single "person". Hw could this be? How was such a combination to be conceived? The first steps towards an understanding had to be negative in character. The wording of the famous Johannine text—"the Word became flesh"—suggests the concept of a transformation of the Word into flesh. But such an idea has only to be clearly formulated to be immediately dismissed. It offends against the basic principle of the perfect and unchangeable nature of the divine. The divine Word cannot cease to be; it cannot be other than it is, namely the divine Word. The idea of a transformation into flesh is unthinkable. Could it be then that Word and flesh coalesce to form some new entity, as gold and silver combine to form electrum, which is something different from either the initial gold or the initial silver? Such an idea offends against the principle of divine immutability as strongly as the first. To quote from St John once again—"that which is born of the flesh is flesh, that which is born of the spirit is spirit". The two are radically distinct. If they come together it cannot be by way of fusion. And so Tertullian is left simply to affirm the combination without any explanation of its nature. The two "substances" retain their respective properties unimpaired. The divine nature is reflected in the miracles, the human nature in the sufferings. One is not transformed into the other, neither do the two coalesce. Yet they do together form a single person.

Origen: a first attempt at explanation

The Church never went back upon that outline sketch. But the Eastern mind was not content to let so boldly paradoxical a picture stand without exploring to the full every avenue of possible interpretation. No one could have been better equipped for the initiation of that task than Origen. Accepting the same outline as Tertullian, Origen develops two further ideas about the nature of the union as aids to understanding. If we speak simply of the co-existence of two "substances" or two natures in the one Christ, then the form of our description suggests the idea of two parallel entities, of two coequal partners. But on any worthy understanding of the nature of the divine this can hardly be seriously intended. If the human and the divine coexist, then the divine must surely be the senior partner. The transformation of the divine into the human is, as Tertullian had claimed, quite unthinkable. But what of a transformation of the human into the divine? Was this equally unthinkable? Or was it not rather the very purpose of the incarnation? Irenaeus had spoken of the Word becoming "what we are that he might bring us to be what he himself is", and the Alexandrian tradition to which Origen belonged spoke freely of man's ultimate destiny as "divinisation". This was never intended to mean that man would be incorporated into the very being of God himself. It was intended to imply rather that man would come to share derivatively in that immortal and changeless perfection, which is characteristic of the divine realm in conspicuous contrast to the human. If that be the ultimate goal of humanity as a whole, must it not have been the more immediate goal for Christ's humanity? At times Origen suggests that this is already happening in the period of the incarnation, that the divinity in Jesus was able to transfigure his body at will so that it would appear differently to different people. At other times—and it was only in this lesser sense that the mind of the Church went with him—such transformation was understood to be effective only in the period after the resurrection. Whatever was to be its form after death, the body of the incarnate Christ was and remained a body like ours. There was no escape therefore from the problem of the two natures. Nevertheless the reminder that those two natures were not simply equals, but that the divine must be in an important sense the ruling factor in such a partnership, was one that was to play an important role in future attempts to understand the nature of their union in the one Christ.

The other important idea in the thought of Origen was the role of Christ's human soul in the union effected by the incarnation. If with St John we speak of the Word becoming flesh (1. 14) or with St Paul we speak of the two natures in terms of "flesh" and "spirit" (e.g. Rom. 1. 3–4), then we are posing the problem in the harshest possible terms. "Word and flesh" or "spirit and flesh" suggest at once the two disparate and incompatible realms of Platonic thought. Their coming together can only be spoken of in terms of sheer paradox or even absurdity. Yet in fact even the Platonist knows in experience of one place where the two realms meet. The human soul belongs in its proper nature to the eternal changeless realm of the ideal forms; that is its true home. Yet however little we can explain it we know from experience that it can be joined with a human body to form the single unity of a personal being. Does not this fact provide an interpretative clue which can offer at least some partial understanding of the apparent paradox or absurdity of an incarnation? In Origen's scheme of thought all rational beings ("logikoi" is the Greek word) were eternal, and derived their rationality and their being from their link with the divine Logos himself. From that perfect state, these rational beings or pre-existent souls had fallen through the abuse of their free-will and so had come to be involved in this world of bodies and of bodily decay—all, that is, except one. One soul had remained from all eternity in a relationship of perfect love and union with the Logos; that soul was the human soul of Jesus. There was no difficulty, Origen argued, in the conception of such a perfect union between a human soul (one of the "logikoi") and the Logos. It was after all the original and proper state of every soul apart from the disruptive influence of sin. Nor was there any difficulty in the idea of a union of soul and body—or at least if difficult to explain it was none the less something of which we had first-hand experience. If therefore we set the human soul of Jesus at the centre of the picture, the idea of the incarnation takes on a new air of intelligibility.

Origen's scheme is a bold and attractive attempt at understanding. Nevertheless, as with his approach to trinitarian thought, it soon ran into serious difficulties. It was not only that Origen's very individual speculations about the pre-existence of all human souls failed to find any

61

general acceptance in the Church. The difficulty which his ideas encountered was more fundamental than that. Origen's scheme spoke of the incarnation as a union of the divine Logos with a whole man complete with rational soul and all the component elements of a normal human existence. This sounded dangerously like the discredited notion of two distinct beings—a full human Jesus and a Christ-spirit or divine Logos. If it was not that, if there was a real union of divine Logos and whole man, then the objection took another form. The kind of union which Origen's scheme described was by its own confession the kind of union which had initially been true of every human soul; it was the kind of union which was true in some degree of every saint and every prophet. The incarnation if understood in such terms is different not in kind but only in degree from the inspiration of other men. Thereby the full divinity of Christ, the basic premiss of Christian worship and of Christian salvation, was felt to be undermined. To focus attention in such a way upon the human soul of Jesus might help to "explain" the incarnation, but it did so only at the cost of explaining away its uniqueness. So the second half of the third century saw the mind of the Church moving firmly away from the kind of explanation that Origen had offered. No alternative emerged. It was simply that men talked, and felt they had no option but to talk, in the directly paradoxical language of a union of Word and flesh.

Such a way of speaking certainly stresses the uniqueness of the incarnation. It also stresses the dominant role of the divine element in the life of Christ. If all talk of a human soul of Jesus is excluded, then it must necessarily be the divine Word himself who was the ruling and directing principle in the life of the incarnate Lord. But such a view had severe difficulties of its own with which to contend. The Church had clearly felt the need to distinguish between the divine and human aspects of Christ's life. But the task had not proved easy. We have seen in Tertullian's talk of the miracles as belonging to the divine nature and the sufferings as belonging to the human the kind of way in which it had been attempted. But once exclude the human soul of Jesus from the picture (as Tertullian emphatically had not done) and the difficulty is greatly increased. "Sufferings of the flesh" is a natural collocation of ideas. If attention could be rigidly restricted to that context the difficulty might not appear insuperable. But it could not be so restricted. The gospels spoke of the experience of emotional disturbance in Christ, of the troubling of his soul at the prospect of his approaching passion (John 12. 27; Matt. 26. 38); they spoke even of his ignorance of the day of the second coming (Mark 13. 32). These things must belong to the sphere of Christ's human nature as surely as his physical sufferings. But how could they be ascribed to the human nature without explicitly affirming the existence of a human soul and allowing it a clear role within the union? Can flesh, literally understood, be ignorant? This was the dilemma which faced those who were determined to keep firmly to the language of Word and flesh, those who felt that no place could be given to Christ's human soul without destroying the uniqueness of the incarnation. It was one aspect of the impact of Arius on the Church that this dilemma was brought clearly and inescapably out into the open.

The Impact of Arius

The nature of the incarnation was not the main issue of debate in the Arian controversy. The main issue, as we saw in the last chapter, was the divine nature of the Son. Was he "god" or "God"? Was he God in the same sense that the Father was God? Was he of the same "ousia" as the Father? But the two questions are most closely tied up with one another. As the earlier second-century apologists had found, if the Word or Son were god only in a secondary

63

sense, the acute philosophical problem of how one was to speak of the changeless, supreme God's self-involvement in the spheres of creation and revelation was greatly eased. Nowhere was that problem more severely felt than in the case of the incarnation. Admittedly there was not the need, as there was with regard to the creation, of arguing that this ought to be thought of as an activity of the Son rather than the Father. That was clearly affirmed by Scripture and universally agreed—except by those discredited Sabellians who tried to maintain that there was no such thing as a real distinction between Son and Father at all. But the nature of the divine self-involvement was so much greater, so much more difficult to accept in the case of the incarnation. Arius argued on philosophical grounds that the Son must be god only in a secondary sense. If one could agree with him, then the problem of the incarnation was very considerably lessened. The divine being who entered into human flesh and accepted the experiences of physical suffering, of emotional disturbance and of ignorance was a lower-level divinity, a god who did not share the "ousia" of God himself. The idea might still be difficult, but at least it was not patently blasphemous and absurd. But if with Athanasius you insist that the Son is "homoousios" with the Father, very God of very God, God in identically the same sense that the Father is God, then the difficulty of the incarnation impinges upon you with a new intensity. Athanasius was not ascribing physical suffering, emotional disturbance and ignorance to the Father, as the Sabellians in effect had done; but he was ascribing them to one who shared all the divine attributes of the Father, one who was God in the same sense that he was God. Was not such a view just as blasphemous, just as absurd as theirs had been? Thus Arius could claim that his belief was not only indispensable for the defence of a true monotheism, but that it was equally essential for preserving the possibility of any intelligible interpretation of the incarnation. In rejecting Arianism as decisively as she did, the Church was forced not only to formulate more clearly her own understanding of the nature of the persons of the godhead. She had also to meet the implicit challenge of Arius with respect to the incarnate Christ.

The reaction to this challenge took very different forms in the two main centres of Christian thought in the East, Alexandria and Antioch. From the time of its foundation by Alexander the Great, Alexandria had been one of the foremost centres of Greek learning in the Eastern world. Antioch, on the other hand, as capital of Syria, was a centre not only of Greek culture but also of Semitic life. Geographically it is a little nearer to the soil of Galilee than Alexandria is; culturally it is a great deal nearer. In the two centres there had grown up distinctive schools of Christian thought with corresponding differences of emphasis. In the interpretation of Scripture, the emphasis of the Antiochenes was laid upon the literal and historical meaning; the Alexandrians were more prone to elaborate mystical and allegorical exegesis of the sacred text. These differences of approach are reflected in their differing reactions to the challenge of Arius.

The Antiochene answer was clear. It was to revive the idea of Christ's human soul as an essential element in any understanding of the person of Christ. This idea had never been explicitly denied. In the Antiochene tradition it had perhaps been dormant rather than dead. In any event Arius, they believed, had shown it to be an essential concept after all. Leave it out of the picture, and the Arian logic is inescapable. If the sole principle of the inner life of the incarnate Christ is the divine Logos himself, then the choice is clear. Either one will have to affirm that "very God of very God" was troubled and ignorant, or one will have to deny with Arius that the Son is God in the fullest meaning of the

65

word. To the Antiochenes either admission appeared as a blasphemous denial of an essential feature of Christian conviction. The answer therefore was obvious. There must have been a human soul in Christ to which the emotional disturbance and the ignorance of which the gospels speak can be ascribed. No other way out seemed possible.

Yet Athanasius, the staunchest anti-Arian of all, did not follow that way. For him, and for those who stood with him in the Alexandrian tradition, the difficulties implicit in such a way out were too great to be borne. To ascribe a human soul to Christ and to make that soul the subject of some of the experiences of the incarnate Lord, this was to split Christ in two; it was to destroy the vitally unique character of the divine act of incarnation. If the life of Christ was a saving life and the death of Christ was a saving death, then the subject of every aspect of that life and death cannot have been other than the divine Word himself. Nothing else would do justice to the religious significance of the life of Christ. How then was Athanasius to escape the Arian dilemma? Was he prepared simply to affirm that the fully divine Word, who is of one substance with the Father, was after all troubled and ignorant? Not as baldly as that or without qualification. Athanasius would have nothing to do with any suggestion of two distinguishable subjects in the Christ; he firmly insists that the divine Word is the sole subject of all the experiences of the incarnate life. But he believed he could escape the horns of the Arian dilemma by insisting that the divine Word acted in differing roles or capacities. The divine Word is the subject of every act and of every experience of the incarnate Christ, but not of them all in the same way. Some things are true of the divine Word in his eternal divine nature, but others are true of him in a different way in virtue of his incarnate status. In becoming incarnate the divine Word did not abandon any of his divine attributes; the suggestion is dismissed as absurd.

But he did assume in addition to them the limitations of his adopted human nature. Thus it was the divine Word who was perturbed at the onset of the passion; but that perturbation was by virtue of his incarnate status and coincided with his remaining changeless and unperturbed in his eternal nature. It was the divine Word who was ignorant of the day of the second coming; but that ignorance was by virtue of his incarnate status and coincided with his remaining omniscient in his eternal nature. It is a less easy and a less clear-cut answer to the challenge of Arius. But it was only an answer of this second kind, so Athanasius believed, that was free from bringing into jeopardy another essential element in Christian faith. So among those who were united in their implacable opposition to Arianism, there grew up two radically opposing lines of thought about the kind of account of the incarnation that needed to be given in a post-Arian age. In due course the Church was to conclude that, different though they were, there was truth in both lines of thought which must be preserved. But before that conclusion could be reached the two approaches were locked in a century of bitter conflict, during which each in turn was developed in opposition to the other to a point at which it drew upon itself the condemnation of the Church as a whole.

Apollinarius

It was the Alexandrian approach which first ran into serious trouble in the person of Apollinarius (c. A.D. 375). He was not in fact himself an Alexandrian. But he was a close friend and fervent admirer of his older contemporary, Athanasius, and their thought was cast in the same basic mould. The see of which he was bishop was Laodicea in Syria. Geographically, therefore, he was in close touch with Antioch and reacted violently against the emphasis on two distinct natures which was characteristic of that school of thought. To speak of the divine Word and a human rational soul co-existing in the one Christ was not just false, he argued, it was meaningless. How could there be two ruling principles linked together in a single person? No proper meaning could be given to such an affirmation. It was a contradiction of what is implicit in the concept of a rational being. But the Antiochenes, in his view, were not merely being muddle-headed. It might not be possible to give any clear meaning to what they were affirming. But it was possible, he claimed, to see that what they were trying to affirm was something hostile to Christian faith, something incompatible with a true idea of Christian salvation. The human mind and will were by nature unstable, fallible and corrupt. No human mind or will could be the author of the salvation which man needed. The only source of salvation was God. What was to be looked for in a saviour, therefore, was the absence of that unstable, fallible and corrupt human mind and its replacement by the divine Word himself. If Christ be the author of the world's salvation, nothing less than that will suffice. If any division between the divine and human aspects in the life of Christ be allowed, then his dying is presumably the first thing that must be allocated to the human side of his experience. But it is into his death that we are baptised; it is his death that is the ground of our hope of salvation. And can the death of a man save us?

So Apollinarius was determined to present the life of the incarnate Christ as a single divine reality through and through. He did not revive those early fanciful theories, which solved the problem by denying in one way or another the reality of the obstinately human elements in which the gospel records abound. What he did do was to take and develop still further the ideas that had been characteristic of his predecessors in the Alexandrian school.

Origen had stressed the directing and transforming role

68

of the divine in relation to the human element in Christ. For Apollinarius that human element consisted only of physical flesh. But the divine Word had taken it into such close union with himself that the two had been forged into a real unity. Such a unity could not alter the unalterable Word; but neither could it leave the flesh unaffected. The transforming power of the divine Word was such that the flesh itself was enabled to share in his divine life-giving properties. Christ's flesh in origin was ordinary human flesh; but by its intimate union with the divine Word it was transformed into divine flesh. That was how it was that Christ's flesh, the most patently human thing about him, could none the less be the life-giving source of salvation, as Christians knew it to be through their reception of it in the eucharist. Word and flesh were one divine reality.

Athanasius had stressed the idea of the divine Word making his own in the incarnation by voluntary self-limitation the restrictive experiences of human existence, so that every experience of the incarnate Christ could rightly be described as in some sense an experience of the divine Word himself. This idea too Apollinarius emphasises and develops. But the idea is much easier to express in general terms than to work out in particular instances. St Luke declares that "Jesus increased in wisdom and stature and in favour with God and man" (2. 52). But what can such words mean if there be no human mind in Christ? Increase in wisdom is equally inapplicable to human flesh and to divine Word. There is only one way in which Apollinarius can give meaning to such a phrase. In the cradle the divine Word allows the fullest scope to those restrictive limitations of human experience which at the incarnation he voluntarily assumes. What St Luke calls a growth in wisdom must therefore really be the divine Word's gradual diminution of the extent of that voluntary self-limitation which he initially accepted when entering

69

the virgin's womb. As the body of Jesus grows, so the divine Word gradually allows an increasing measure of his infinite wisdom to find appropriate expression. In Gethsemane Jesus prayed, "Not my will but thine be done" (Luke 22. 42). But if the only will in Christ be that of the divine Son himself, who is very God of very God, can there be two conflicting wills between God and his Son, between very God and very God? Of course not, says Apollinarius; indeed there is no question of two wills at all. It is one and the same will expressing itself on the one hand in recognition of the self-imposed limitations of the incarnation and on the other hand in its fully divine capacity.

Apollinarius, I said above, did not revive those early fanciful theories which upheld the full divinity of Christ by denying the evidence of his full humanity. It is difficult not to feel that in the detailed out-working of his ideas he comes at times very close to such a revival. That was how it seemed also to his Antiochene contemporaries. His theory, they complained, involved the mutilation of Christ's divinity and of his humanity at every point. Divinity that could be so completely and directly joined to human flesh was divinity degraded. Humanity that had no mind, humanity that was made up of flesh alone—and divine life-giving flesh at that—was no genuine humanity.

Serious though these criticisms were and are, they were not the ones which were of primary importance in securing the Church's repudiation of Apollinarian teaching. The primary concern of Apollinarius in the development of his ideas was his desire to give an account of the person of Christ which would measure up to man's need of a saviour. Only in his terms, he argued, could it be claimed that the divine Word had entered right into and taken saving control of the human situation. If adequacy for the requirements of man's salvation was the touch-stone to which Apollinarius appealed in commending his ideas, by that touchstone let him also be judged. That it was the divine Word, very God of very God, who was incarnate in Jesus, and that nothing less was adequate if he were to be man's saviour, was not in dispute. That was common ground to all opponents of Arianism. But there was another principle not to be forgotten in any discussion of what was needed for man's salvation. Salvation needs not only God as its author; it needs man as its recipient. Irenaeus and Tertullian had insisted on that fact in their defence of Christ's humanity almost two centuries before. In their case the nub of the argument had been the reality or otherwise of Christ's physical body. But they had applied the same principle to the other aspects of his human nature also. With all the concern about how to give an adequate account of the unity of Christ's person, this line of reasoning had been largely neglected and forgotten. But now that Apollinarius had come out into the open with an explicit denial of Christ's possession of a rational, human soul, it was quickly and forcefully resurrected. It was given classic expression in some words of Gregory of Nazianzus: "What is not assumed is not healed." The sin of Adam was not simply a sin of the flesh, but of the mind; as Apollinarius readily agreed, it is at the level of his inner being that man needs to be redeemed. But if that be so, it was argued in reply, then if Christ did not possess a human mind or a human soul, he fails to meet man at his point of greatest need.

But to say that Apollinarius was wrong was not to say that the Antiochenes were right. Apollinarius stood in the Alexandrian tradition, but in his explicit denial of Christ's human soul he had clearly developed that tradition in a more extreme form than those who had gone before him. To repudiate his teaching did not mean to repudiate the whole tradition in which he stood. Moreover, to assert that Christ must have had a human soul for our human souls to

71

be saved did nothing to overcome the difficulties that had long been felt about every attempt to give an account of Christ's person which allowed place there not only for the divine Logos himself but for a human soul as well. The difficulties inherent in the Alexandrian tradition had been clearly exposed, but if one looked in the same critical spirit at Antiochene teaching, might not equally damaging cracks appear in that structure also?

Theodore and Nestorius

The teaching of Apollinarius was condemned at the Council of Constantinople in 381. It was exactly fifty years before a form of the Antiochene teaching met with a similar condemnation at the Council of Ephesus in 431. That fifty years coincides almost exactly with the active teaching life of the greatest of all the Antiochenes, Theodore of Mopsuestia, who was ordained about 383 and died in 428. In Theodore's teaching the full humanity of Jesus, body and soul, is clearly affirmed as a distinguishable entity within the one Christ. The Antiochenes had insisted all along that such a distinction was essential if the threat of Arianism was to be kept safely at bay. And now they had the further example of Apollinarius to reinforce upon their minds the inescapable necessity of such an emphasis. But this stress was very much more than just a necessary escape device to avoid the twin perils of Arian and Apollinarian heresy. Theodore's understanding of the person of Christ has just as positive a character as that of Apollinarius and one that is just as closely related to the needs of man's salvation.

Apollinarius had seen in the freedom of the human will a liability to sin so fundamental that it had to be totally eliminated from the person of the saviour and replaced by the infallible will of the divine Logos himself. Theodore does not deny the reality of man's involvement in the disharmonies of a sinful world. But he sees man's freedom, whose abuse is admittedly the ground of his sin and of his guilt, as being also the potential source of his moral growth. It is in and through the proper exercise of that freedom that God's intended purpose for mankind is to be fulfilled. And it is precisely that which had already happened in the person of Christ. In the perfect obedience of his fully human life the intention of God's creation of mankind has been achieved. When Theodore ascribes the temptations in the wilderness or the struggle in the garden of Gethsemane to the human soul of Jesus, he is not motivated simply by a desire to avoid at any cost the seeming blasphemy of ascribing such a thing to the divine Logos; he is not simply accepting the only alternative left to him in view of the unconvincing nature of the kind of explanation which Athanasius and Apollinarius had found themselves forced to give of such events. The triumph of the human will of Jesus over temptation in the wilderness and in Gethsemane is of the very essence of what it means to call Christ saviour. He is the high priest who meets the needs of man just because he "was in all points tempted like as we are, yet without sin" (Heb. 4. 15); he is the forerunner, whose triumphant finishing of the course is the assurance that others will be able to complete it victoriously also.

Is Theodore then wanting to paint Christ simply as the perfect man, who by his own moral strength has avoided sin and won his way to heaven? If that were all he had intended to affirm, he would have found no place in the Church of the post-Arian age. Christ was not only fully man with a fully human nature, he was also the divine Word, very God with a fully divine nature. The human nature existed in a perfect and unique association with the divine Word. The human choices and triumphs were genuine human choices and genuine human triumphs; but they were not exclusively or independently human achievements. They were the fruit of that perfect obedience, that

73

perfect association with the divine Word which was true of Christ's human soul at every moment of its existence. What then was the nature of this perfect association of divine Word and human soul? Was it substantially different from the kind of association which is true of the great prophet or the great saint? For there also it would be natural to speak of making genuine human choices, choices which are not exclusively or independently the saint's, but rather the fruit of his obedience, the fruit of his intimate association with the divine Word. It was always the fear of Athanasius and those who thought in similar terms that to allow a full human nature with a rational human soul to the incarnate Christ must inevitably reduce the incarnation to a special case of prophethood or sainthood. Theodore admits that the association of Word and soul in Christ is of the same kind as that known in the experience of prophet or saint, but claims that they are totally different in degree. What other kind of association could it be? Metaphysical terms, such as "ousia", seemed to him totally inappropriate. At the fundamental level of being God is omnipresent. To describe the union of the divine Word and the human soul of Jesus in such terms would be to circumscribe the being of God in a way that was unthinkable. Moral or spiritual categories were the only ones appropriate to the subject. It is only in such terms that the union can meaningfully be described. The word that Theodore particularly uses is a word from the song of the angels who declared to the shepherds the good news of Christ's birth, the word translated "favour" or "good pleasure". It is a union of God's pleasure, a union of perfect moral harmony, a union of the kind that can only exist when the perfect love of God meets with a response of loving obedience from man. But if this seems to reduce Christ to the level of prophet or saint, the absolute difference in degree must not be overlooked. The union in Christ's case was perfect and complete at every moment.

It was true of him from the very start of his life; it was true indeed from the very time of his conception. A union of so permanent and so complete a character seemed to Theodore to do full justice to that uniqueness to which the Scriptures and Christian tradition testified. Indeed it was nothing less than a unity of person.

But having spoken so freely of the two, of the divine Word, the second person of the godhead, and the man whom he assumed in the incarnation (for Theodore regularly speaks in such personal terms of Christ's human nature), was it really possible for him to speak in equally convincing terms of their unity, of Christ as a single person? Of course it was perfectly possible to find a word to use when speaking of the union of the two. The Word which Theodore used, the word usually translated person, was the Greek word "prosopon". But how much did it really mean? It certainly did not mean what we would mean by unity of personality, unity of inner being. The divine Word and a human soul could not coalesce to form one single entity in that sense without involving the hated idea of a commingling of the divine and human, the idea of which Apollinarius had been guilty. Nor on the other hand did it mean a unity of mere appearance, a unity which was only a seeming and not something real. It must stand somewhere between these two extremes. It must imply a unity that is real but which belongs to the outward aspect rather than the inner being of the person, a unity that still allows for a clear distinction between those acts and experiences which are properly acts or experiences of the divine Word and those which are properly acts or experiences of the human soul.

But as with the thought of Apollinarius, so here also the real difficulty of the concept emerges most clearly when we move away from the general formula and see what it involves when worked out in particular detail. St John records Jesus as saying to his disciples: "I came forth from

75

the Father and am come into the world: again I leave the world and go to the Father" (16. 28). But who is the real speaker? Who is the "I" of whom the verse speaks? Theodore looks at the first clause and insists that the "I" can only be the divine Word himself. There was no pre-existent divine-human Christ. The only being who could truly say that he came forth from the Father is the divine Word himself as distinct from the human nature which he assumed at the incarnation. But then he looks at the second half of the verse—"I leave the world and go to the Father." Such a saying, he argues, cannot be a saying of the divine Word. For the divine Word never leaves the world which he has made and which he continually sustains; he cannot go to the Father when he is eternally one with him. The "I" of that second clause must be Christ's human nature, the man who by his union with the Word is to be brought through death, resurrection and ascension to the very presence of the Father himself. In the first clause the Word speaks; in the second the man. And in similar vein many other of the sayings from the gospels are divided up and apportioned carefully to the appropriate partner in that union which is Christ. If Apollinarius' explanation of many of the gospel texts is forced and harsh, so also is Theodore's. Little wonder that his opponents came in time to accuse him of teaching not one Christ, but two sons—a divine Son of God and a human son of man.

Theodore died, honoured and revered, in 428. Within three years his former pupil, Nestorius, had been condemned at the Council of Ephesus. Apollinarius' condemnation was the outcome of his developing the Alexandrian tradition to a stage beyond that of any of its earlier exponents by his explicit denial of Christ's human soul. It is natural to look for some comparable development of the Antiochene tradition in the teaching of Nestorius which would account for his rapid and permanent downfall. But one looks in vain. There is nothing in the teaching of Nestorius that is significantly different from that of his predecessor, Theodore. The difference between them lies not in their teaching but in their situations. Theodore was the scholarly bishop of an obscure see; Nestorius was an outspoken, reforming preacher and archbishop of Constantinople, the capital of the Eastern world and chief rival to Alexandria for the leadership of the Eastern churches. Moreover it has been few men's fate to be faced with so able and so unscrupulous an adversary as Cyril of Alexandria, with whom Nestorius had to contend. The story of the condemnation of Nestorius belongs more to the story of ecclesiastical rivalries than to that of early Christian thought. But this much it did show clearly. The discrediting of Apollinarius did not mean the acceptance of traditional Antiochene teaching as embodying an understanding of the person of Christ precisely acceptable to the whole Church. The weaknesses of each tradition had been exposed. What positive convictions remained which would do justice to the mind of the Church as a whole?

The Chalcedonian Definition

The Alexandrian tradition had stood for the priority of the divine element in the incarnate life of Christ, so that the incarnation could be clearly seen to be a divine initiative, a divine act through and through. At first this emphasis had seemed to exclude the possibility of allowing to Christ the possession of a human soul. But such a denial had come to be regarded universally as false; Christ had a full human nature, body and rational soul. But within the confines of that admission, the Alexandrians were still free to assert the priority of the divine Word, to see him as the subject of all the experiences of the incarnate Christ. Cyril of Alexandria, like most of those who stood in that same tradition, thought in Platonist terms. It was natural there-

77

fore for him to stress the universal nature of Christ's humanity. "What is not assumed is not healed"; the Alexandrians had accepted that lesson. The important thing about Christ therefore was not that the Word had become a man but that the Word had assumed humanity in order to save it. If that were the vital purpose in affirming Christ's full humanity, how could it be better done than by asserting his assumption not of individual but of universal manhood? For Cyril as a Platonist such language carried no overtones of unreality. The universal was always more real for the Platonist than any particular instance of it. By speaking in this way, Cyril could feel that he was doing full justice to the wholeness and to the reality of Christ's human nature, and yet avoid having to regard that human nature as a second, alternating subject in the life of the one Christ. For the human nature of Christ was humanity at large, not an individual man who must be thought of as the subject of particular experiences. Thus the Alexandrian could continue to assert that it was the divine Word who suffered and died on the cross for man's salvation, provided he added the qualification (which he was perfectly ready to do) that he did so by virtue of his incarnate status and that he remained all the while impassible and immortal in his eternal being. Some people in the Church would not like such a bold way of speaking, but the Church as a whole did not wish to say that it was false or improper to do so.

The Antiochene tradition had always wished to stress the presence of the two natures in Christ. This too received the approval of the Church at large. After the condemnation of Nestorius, some of the more extreme exponents of the Alexandrian tradition had tried to insist that while it was perfectly proper to speak of Christ as made up from the two natures, divine and human, it was not permissible to speak of those two natures continuing to exist in the incarnate life. Once the two had been united in the incarnation, it was argued, one should speak only of one nature. But such ideas were rejected and their chief advocate, Eutyches, condemned. If one were to speak of one nature only in the incarnate life, one must be implying either the exclusion of the human nature or an illicit mixing or fusion of the two. All such notions had been discarded long ago. The language of two natures was accepted; it was only talk of two Sons, which had never been intended, that was forbidden. So the Antiochene could continue to speak of the divine Word and the human soul of Jesus as the source of the appropriately distinguished activities of the incarnate life, provided he added the qualification (which he was perfectly ready to do) that they never acted in isolation or independence of one another, but always in the closest conceivable conjunction and association with each other. Again there would be those in the Church who would object to such ways of talking, but the Church as a whole was not prepared to disallow them.

These two traditions could not be combined into a single coherent picture. But there was a considerable measure of common ground between them. At an official level all that could be done was to try to define that common ground, to show the limits within which any account of the person of Christ must remain if it were to be true to the thought of the Church as a whole. This was the function of the famous "Chalcedonian definition" agreed at the Council of Chalcedon in 451.

"We confess one and the same our Lord Jesus Christ, the same perfect in godhead, the same perfect in manhood, truly God and truly man, the same of a rational soul and body . . . acknowledged in two natures, without confusion, without change, without division, without separation, the difference of the natures being by no means taken away because of the union but rather the distinctive character of each nature being preserved and combining in one person (prosopon) or entity (hypostasis)."

It was a clear compromise. The Alexandrians had traditionally protested that to describe the unity of Christ as one of "prosopon" was to use so loose a term as to suggest it was not a real unity at all. The Antiochenes had similarly objected that to describe it as one of "hypostasis" was to use so tight a term as to leave no room for the continuing distinction of natures. The difference is solved by treating the two terms as simple equivalents. Like all such compromises it failed to satisfy the extremists of either party. Political and nationalist factors may have been the primary causes, but doctrinal discontent contributed its share to the breakaway of the Nestorian churches of Persia and the Monophysite (one nature only) churches of Egypt and Ethiopia after the Council of Chalcedon.

But for the majority it was, and has remained, a normative statement guiding the Church in all her subsequent attempts to understand more fully the person of Christ. It is not itself such an understanding. Rather it limits the range of acceptable understandings, while still leaving room for a variety of accounts that will differ from one another in the detail of their outworking. As an answer to the problems of its day it is one for which we have reason to be grateful. In an age which, unlike our own, started from an unhesitating conviction in the full divinity of Christ, it insisted that his full humanity must be affirmed with equal force. Moreover, it left room for this to be done not only in the generalised Alexandrian form of a universal human nature but also in the more individualised, historical mode of Antiochene thought. Had it not done so, it is difficult to see how there could have been a genuine continuity of tradition between the age of the Fathers and our own historically conscious age.

But if we go on to ask whether the formula of Chalcedon

has the same kind of direct value as a normative guide for our own day which it has rightly had in the past, we must give a more qualified answer. The Fathers thought in terms of the union of a perfect divine and a perfect human nature. But do we know the meaning of either term in that union? Indeed are we even sure that the concept of a perfect human nature is a concept that has any meaning at all? Moreover when the Fathers went on to speak of that union of natures as a union into one "person", they did not mean what we would mean by a psychological unity of personality. That was not the way in which the issue posed itself to them; but to us it is. We cannot convince ourselves today by talk of a unity of person which does not even raise the question of the psychological unity of personality.

We have seen how difficult it was for either the fully-fledged Apollinarian or the fully-fledged Nestorian to give a convincing account of the particular words and acts of the Jesus of the gospel story. But it is no easier for the fully-fledged Chalcedonian. The "Chalcedonian Definition" itself does not even attempt to do so; that was not its task. It sets out simply to provide the limits within which the task, if it is to be attempted at all, must be done. Remaining true to Chalcedon has often been described as being like keeping along a narrow ridge between two chasms, the chasms of Apollinarian and Nestorian heresy. But we cannot be content to spend all our days in the rarefied atmosphere of the ridge. We have to look for a way down off the ridge which will lead into a more fruitful valley than either the Apollinarian or the Nestorian chasm. We cannot be sure that there is a way down which we will be able to find; the gospel records may not be designed to serve as a guide to the kind of path which we want to take; they don't always provide the material needed to answer the kind of question which we cannot help asking. But that does not absolve us from making the attempt.

The form in which the problem of Christ's person forces itself on us today is not one to which the witness of Chalcedon was designed to provide the answer. We have to struggle with the same fundamental question with which the Fathers were struggling. How can this Jesus, with all the marks of manhood upon him, be the one in whom God saves the world? But we have to learn to struggle with it in our terms and not in theirs. We have to use in the struggle, as for the most part they tried to do, all the insights of contemporary philosophy and psychology without becoming the slave of any. Amidst the difficulties and uncertainties of that task, Chalcedon will remain as a valuable link with the past; but it should not be treated as an anchor, which would keep us not only linked with the past but still living in it.

Chapter Four

SIN AND SALVATION

THE modern reader who turns, without knowledge of their historical context, to the Athanasian creed or the Chalcedonian Definition is likely to jump to the conclusion that their authors must have been academic theologians, whose concern was the construction of detailed schemes of intellectual orthodoxy bearing only the most remote relation to the realities of the spiritual life. The last two chapters should have sufficed to show that such a picture is a caricature of the Christian Fathers. They were men who whatever their faults—and they were many—were passionately concerned to lay hold of and to propagate the gospel of salvation. This was their dominant concern, it was this that drove them on step by step in their task of doctrinal definition. The full divinity of the divine Word must be maintained whatever the intellectual difficulties, because only so could he be man's saviour. Alexandrian and Antiochene alike defended their differing traditions of Christ's person on the same basic ground; the things upon which they were each insisting were things which, it seemed to them, must be true if Christ were to be saviour of mankind. If this then were so dominant a concern for them, we do well to go on and ask how they understood that salvation. What was the nature of this primary human need for salvation? What did the coming of Christ into the world do to meet it?

One of the outstanding works of the age of the Fathers sets out to answer this very question. In most of his extant writings Athanasius' overriding aim is to demonstrate the errors of Arian teaching. But in a book entitled *On the Incarnation of the Word* Athanasius sets out in positive terms the reasons for the incarnation and the way in which it effects the divine plan for man's salvation. It is not a long work, rather less than half the length of this book. One can see why the man who wrote it, the man who thought as its author thought, would be an implacable foe of Arianism. But there is no mention of that great struggle in the book itself. For that reason it has most commonly been regarded as a work of Athanasius' early youth, from a date just before the outbreak of the great Arian controversy in A.D. 318. It would be a remarkably mature work if really written by one so young, and there is no reason why all explicit reference to the controversy should not have been deliberately omitted from a work primarily intended to make the central ideas of the Christian faith intelligible to the pagan world. Be that as it may, the work is one which gives in clear outline an account of man's sin and of God's salvation, an account which is generally representative of the thought of the Fathers as a whole. A brief summary of its argument is the best approach to the subject of the present chapter.

Man was created out of nothing in the image of God; he is not by nature immortal, but he was created so that it was possible for him to progress to an immortal fellowship with God through contemplation of the divine Word. But men fell away from their divinely intended destiny through sin. The outcome of that sin was twofold. One result was blindness; man lost the knowledge of God which had been open to him, so that the creation became something which veiled God rather than revealed him. But the second result was something still more radical. It meant a return, in accordance with God's explicit judgment upon sin, to that death, that corruption, that non-existence from which God in his love had originally called man forth and created him. To meet this need of man the Word of God became incarnate, and that incarnation meets man's need in a threefold way.

In the first place by the mere fact of the incarnation, new life is introduced into the world. The Word was the agent of the original creation, but man had proved too weak to hold on to what had there been given him or to progress to his intended destiny. By the fact of the incarnation this link between the divine and the human is re-established in a more secure manner. The Word, being fully divine and fully united to man in the incarnation, can impart the divine life to him without fear of its being lost once more.

But furthermore, by taking a human body, he revealed to men in their blindness an image of the invisible God in a form directly accessible to the human senses. By his life, his words and his works he restored to them their lost knowledge of God. This was the importance of the period of the ministry. Incarnation, death and resurrection might appear to be the only essential redemptive occasions; but the ministry had also its part to play in meeting man's need for the knowledge of God.

Finally Christ's death was a debt of justice which had to be paid. God did not wish his own creation to fall back into corruption and death, but neither could he be untrue to the law which he himself had laid down. So for man to be freed from corruption, the law requiring death had to be met. It was justly met by Christ because in view of his representative humanity all men could be reckoned to have died in him. And those who could be reckoned to have died in him must similarly be regarded as rising with him above the level of that corruption into which they had fallen.

These then are the fundamental ways in which the incarnation meets our human need—the impartation of divine life, the mediation of the knowledge of God, the payment of the debt of death and its conquest in resurrection. In one of the closing sections of the book (54), as Athanasius draws in the threads of his argument, all these ideas appear together in concise and summary form: "He was made human that we might be made divine; he manifested himself by a body that we might receive the idea of the unseen Father; he endured the insolence of men that we might inherit immortality."

Sin lies at the root of man's problem. But sin gives rise to blindness and to mortality. These three, ignorance, mortality and sin, are closely interrelated, each continually enhancing and reinforcing the influence of the other. Each was widely recognised as expressing a fundamental aspect of man's predicament. None is ever regarded as exclusive of the other, but the emphasis is put on different aspects by varying writers and at varying times. While recognising the dangers involved in any such separation, we may adopt this threefold division in our attempt to describe more fully the Fathers' understanding of man's basic need.

1. *Ignorance*

"My people are destroyed for lack of knowledge," says the Old Testament prophet (Hos. 4. 6). The word is used absolutely, though it is clearly the practical knowledge of God and of his will that is meant. Jesus had defined the very purpose of his mission to the world as bringing men to a knowledge of the one true God (John 17. 3). In the Greek world also knowledge was among the most coveted goals of human aspiration. That the word had for the Greek ear a more theoretical sense than for the Hebrew is perfectly true. But it would be wrong to regard the transition as one from a religious to an intellectual meaning of the term. Knowledge was the philosopher's goal; but philosophy was as much a way of life as an intellectual discipline. Moreover, the initiate in the mystery cults was also in search of knowledge or illumination. The knowledge for which the Greek world longed was not identical in meaning with the knowledge of which the Hebrew prophet spoke, but it was still at heart a knowledge of God. It was therefore a natural emphasis in the teaching of the Apologists to stress the Christian gospel as the curing of man's blindness, the overcoming of man's ignorance of God. Had not Paul himself told the philosophically minded people of Athens that he could remove the ignorance with which they worshipped "the Unknown God" (Acts 17. 23)?

In speaking of Christ the second-century Apologists thought of him primarily as the Logos, the Word or Reason of God. It is the function of a word to instruct; it is the function of reason to enlighten the mind. It was therefore natural for them to present Christ as the one who had brought to the world the teaching of that knowledge and that truth towards which the minds of men so eagerly and so ineffectually groped. Listen to the evangelistic appeal which comes towards the close of Clement of Alexandria's work entitled *An Exhortation to the Heathen*: "Receive Christ, receive sight, receive thy light 'that you may know well both God and man' (a phrase quoted from Homer's *Iliad*) . . . let us put away ignorance and oblivion of the truth, and removing the darkness which obstructs as dimness of sight let us contemplate the only true God."

Baptism, the rite of initiation by which anyone responding to Clement's appeal would be brought into the Christian fellowship, is a rite with a wide range of association and with a great richness of imagery. Yet the name by which the Fathers most commonly speak of it is a name which is in no way linked with the imagery of the rite itself. "Illumination" in the writings of the Fathers means simply baptism; the "illuminands" are the catechumens, and the "illuminated" the baptised. The terms came naturally; as the moment of response to Christ, baptism was supremely the moment of illumination in which the light of saving knowledge is imparted.

This understanding of man's need and of Christ's salvation continued as an important element in the thought of the Fathers throughout. Never again was it as dominant an element as it was in the thought of the early Apologists. Even there it never stood alone. Light and life go always closely together. When Jesus spoke of bringing men to a knowledge of the one true God he identified that knowledge with life eternal. Paul did not regard his sermon on the Areopagus as being complete without explicit reference to the resurrection. The Logos who was teacher of the mind and enlightener of the reason was also the Logos which mediated between the immortal divine realm and the transient world of men. And in this respect, as Gregory of Nyssa was to put it: "The manner of our salvation owes its efficacy less to instruction by teaching than to what he who entered into fellowship with man actually did."

There were those who claimed that illumination or knowledge was all that man needed. But that claim was one of the very things that separated them off from the main body of orthodox Christians. Such people— Gnostics, as they were called from the Greek word "gnosis", meaning knowledge—believed that the real man was a spiritual being, lost and astray from his true home in an alien material environment. His need is simply to be woken from his slumbers, to be shown who and what he really is. Salvation is receiving the lost knowledge of oneself. For man, if he but knew it, is a spiritual nature, an imperishable denizen of the heavenly realm. But even the Gnostic could not fail to speak also in terms of man's mortality. The material world of bodily existence might

88

not be man's true home, but it was the situation in which he now found himself. Knowledge of himself was saving knowledge precisely because it showed him that in his true nature he was superior to and free from the world of corruption and death. Moreover, in the view of most Gnostics, it was not true of all men that they were of pure heavenly origin. Some were—those some being usually identified with the members of the particular exclusive Gnostic sect itself. For them certainly nothing more was needed for salvation than the disclosure of their true nature. But there were others who belonged to a lesser order of creation. Some indeed belonged so completely to this lower realm that they were incapable of salvation. But there was a third group who stood between the other two— neither pure spiritual beings by nature nor totally incapable of becoming such. They were in need of something more akin to the normal Christian view of salvation if they were to be rescued from their present condition.

2. *Mortality*

The origins of Gnosticism is one of the great issues of debate between scholars at the present time. There can be little doubt that one factor in its growth was the religious development in a pessimistic form of the popularised Platonism of the age. The Platonist world-view with its two realms, the eternal world of the ideal forms and the changing world of the senses, naturally lent itself to development of this kind. In the Gnostic view there was the eternal realm, to which belong truth and peace, life and immortality, while the realm of the temporal world is characterised by error and anxiety, death and decay. There is an upper world in which are to be found true being and eternal life; but men are shut away from that world in the realm of becoming which leads only to frustration and to death. This mood of despair (a mood not unlike that of some modern existentialist writing) was a feature of the age in a way that had not been true of the earlier, more creative stages of Greek civilisation. To those who thought in this way, salvation must consist in deliverance from the realm of decay and translation into the realm of immortality, rescue from the world below and rebirth into the world above. The Gnostic who looked to Christ for a salvation of this kind was looking for a Christ who belonged exclusively to the world of pure being. The world of becoming, the world of change, was the very thing from which he was to save them; he would be no saviour if he had become fully involved, and therefore entrapped, in that world himself. Gnostics were amongst those, therefore, who insisted most strongly on the exclusively divine nature of the Christ. He was, for them, a divine being belonging entirely to the divine realm. The salvation that he brought was to transfer men altogether out of this world into that upper realm.

In this extreme form the picture was not one which the Church could acknowledge as a true account either of man's need or of God's salvation. The physical realm, the world of the senses, was the good creation of God; it was not itself evil, not the very root of man's trouble, not something in which the saviour could not have shared. Nevertheless, despite this deep and fundamental difference of outlook, the mind of the Church did not stand in direct and unqualified opposition to that of the Gnostics. Her attitude to the created world was ambivalent. It was the good creation of God—certainly. But it was not his last word in creation. As we have already seen from the outline sketch of Athanasius' *On the Incarnation,* man was not created immortal but he was created for immortality. The world that should have revealed God now veiled him. The mortality, which should have been the starting-point of man's growth, had now become the irrevocable sentence of his death. Finitude and mortality were therefore things that in practice stood over man's life and threatened it. It was necessary that man should receive salvation from them. The language in which many of the Fathers spoke of that salvation is language that falls strangely on our ears. 2 Peter, probably the last of all the New Testament books to be written, speaks of Christians as escaping "the corruption that is in the world" and "becoming partakers of the divine nature" (1. 4). Emboldened by such language the Fathers spoke freely of men being given a share in the divine nature, or more boldly still of men being made divine. The unfamiliarity of the language makes the more important a careful consideration of its intended meaning.

We have already met with the famous saying of Irenaeus that "the Word became what we are that he might bring us to be even what he is himself". On another occasion he speaks of God making us "at first merely men, and then at length gods". But he does not see this as involving a simple rejection of the human or as a reversal of God's original intention; he sees it rather as two stages in a single divine plan. The Word, who in the incarnation became what we are in order to make us what he is, is the same Word which was operative in the original creation, the one in whose image the first man was made. Adam was created an innocent child, intended to grow up into the full image and likeness of God. That development was arrested by man's sin and by the death that follows from it. But at the incarnation the development is set in motion once again; a new and firmer link is established between man and the divine life; the Word continues his creative work in a way which will no longer be thwarted. Irenaeus makes his point forcefully by drawing a distinction between the image and the likeness of God which was certainly not the intention of the original text. Adam was made at the beginning simply in the image of God, a man;

at the end he will have grown also into the likeness of God and become a god. His divinisation is the fulfilment rather than the negation of his humanity, as manhood is the fulfilment rather than the negation of childhood. His becoming a god was never intended to suggest his becoming an additional member of the Trinity. It was intended to imply his entry into the eternal and immortal realm of being, in the closest possible relation and assimilation to God which can be conceived but one which falls clearly short of a relation of identity.

Man needs salvation from his mortality. That is assured to him by the very fact of the incarnation. The gap between the two worlds has been bridged. Divine nature has taken hold of human nature and given to it the prospect of immortality. But Irenaeus had always the errors of the Gnostics in view as he wrote. He was determined to stress that this salvation was a salvation of humanity not from humanity, a salvation of the world not from the world, a salvation of the body not from the body. Any picture of salvation which would make this point unmistakably clear was attractive to him. He affirms the millenarian hope of a thousand year reign by Christ on a renewed and rejuvenated earth, which finds expression in the Book of Revelation and was a popular idea with many second-century Christians. But this was not a notion which established itself in the consciousness of the Church as a whole after his time. The Eastern church was in general prepared to spiritualise the notion away. It did find a greater measure of support in the West for a time. Its effective disappearance from the future hopes of the main body of the Church came when Augustine reinterpreted the millennium as referring to the present era of the Church—by then become the dominant faith of men throughout the known world.

More significant was Irenaeus' insistence on the resurrection of the body, the resurrection of man's actual physical flesh. The idea was full of difficulties, a source of scorn and ridicule in the eyes of those cultured pagans whom the Christians were anxious to convince. Was it something desirable at all? they asked. What is the point of teeth and all the rest of the paraphernalia of digestion when there is to be no more eating and drinking? What is the point of resurrecting the sexual organs when there is to be no marrying or giving in marriage? Is it indeed even something conceivable? How is the cannibal to give back on resurrection day the flesh of those whose bodies he has eaten and which has become incorporated into his own? The Fathers were not unaware of these problems. They agreed that the flesh would have to undergo a process of transformation; as they are now "flesh and blood cannot inherit the kingdom of God" (1 Cor. 15. 50); they must somehow be freed from that corruption and decay which necessarily characterise all flesh in our present existence. Nevertheless they were insistent that in some way or another the same physical substance which is man's now would be his also in the resurrection. Man was not just a spirit enclosed in a foreign and alien envelope of flesh. He was body and soul. Christ had become man with a physical body too. It was part of the logic of an incarnational faith, of faith in the Word made flesh, that that same flesh should participate in the salvation that he brought. On this issue Irenaeus was no lone voice. What he thought, the Fathers as a whole thought after him. The lone voice in this instance, but a voice deserving to be heard none the less, was the voice of Origen.

The thought of Origen stands somewhere in between that of Irenaeus and that of the Gnostics. He did not, with the Gnostics, see the body simply as evil and man's salvation as a direct escape from it. He did, with Irenaeus, see man's destiny as a divinisation, as a development from

93

his present condition. But it is for him a growth away from the human in which the physical will ultimately be eliminated. The incarnation was not the eternal consecration of the material. It was rather the necessary means of God's condescension in reaching down to us at the point where we are. Shut off as we are in the realm of becoming, we were in no position to contemplate the eternal Word in his pure and proper form. But it is our destiny to do so. The incarnation is only the starting-point. When we have first met the divine Word there, we must gradually be weaned from those beginnings. It is as the mind passes beyond the material realm altogether and engages upon contemplation of the divine Word as he is in himself and apart from the incarnation altogether that the goal of our divinisation will be achieved. In developing his thought about the resurrection, Origen bases his ideas closely on the Pauline conception of the seed (1 Cor. 15). The physical body is the seed which is to grow into the flower of a spiritual existence in which the physical will be done away altogether. The physical is not simply repudiated; it is the seed from which the spiritual grows; but for the flower to grow the seed must die and disappear. With much of the mystical spirituality of Origen's approach the Church was in cordial agreement; indeed she was greatly indebted to it for the development of her thought upon that topic; but to any denial of the permanent resurrection of the flesh she remained implacably opposed.

The Church's answer to the problem of man's mortality which we have considered so far is one that was centred on the incarnation. At the incarnation divine and human natures met, and human nature as a whole received an injection of immortality. It was a way of thought congenial to those who, like the Alexandrians, thought in terms of natures as real entities. Cyril of Alexandria, as we have seen, found it essential to an adequate understanding of the unity of Christ's person to insist on the universal, as opposed to the individual, character of his human nature. That same emphasis on the universal nature of Christ's humanity fitted well with a presentation of the incarnation as the antidote to the universal problem of man's mortality. But even for such thinkers the equally obvious relevance of Christ's resurrection was never forgotten. And for those who like the Antiochenes stressed rather the individual character of Christ's humanity, it was his resurrection which was the main emphasis.

No writer stresses the problem of man's mortality more strongly than the great Antiochene scholar, Theodore of Mopsuestia. The achievement of virtue, he argues, requires that men should think and act in the light of eternity. But our mortality makes us think only in terms of this life; it narrows our vision and restricts our aspirations; thereby it leads us into sin. This is something that will remain with man inevitably until this life is over. But in Christ we can see the pledge of man's victory over mortality. The human element in Christ, that whole man which the divine Word assumed at the incarnation, has by his intimate association with the Word been brought through death to resurrection and the very presence of God himself. And the Spirit which he gives to us is the spirit of life, the spirit of promise, the pledge of our future immortality. To live in the Spirit is to live in the light of the future, a future that has already been realised in Christ and which will therefore in due time be ours also. It is therefore to be freed from the paralysing grip of man's mortality.

3. *Sin*

The Greek Fathers have often been criticised for regarding mortality, man's finitude, as the root problem instead of human sin. They do see mortality as a very important aspect of the human predicament, and one that must be viewed and dealt with in its own right. But they never see it as something existing in independence of human sin. The fact that mortality can be an important cause of human sin is never exclusive of the correlative idea that sin is the cause of man's mortality. "Death entered into the world by sin" (Rom. 5. 12). There were many differing theories as to how that could be so. But the fact itself was not in dispute. Behind, and continuing alongside, the problem of man's mortality was the problem of his sin.

Origen, as so often, had a solution all his own to explain the link between mortality and sin, a solution closely corresponding to his understanding of the nature of man's eventual resurrection life. In Origen's view, all rational souls have existed from eternity. It would not be consonant either with God's nature or with theirs that they should undergo a beginning of existence. But bodily existence is altogether another matter. That only came to be as a result of the sin of those pre-existent souls. If this seems to suggest a picture of the body as necessarily evil, a view that is Gnostic rather than Christian, there is this to be said in Origen's defence. Bodily existence may be a punishment for sin, but it is reformatory rather than simply retributive in intention. The body is not simply evil; it is a divinely intended spur to the soul to help it win its way back again to an eternal, spiritual existence in the heavenly realm. For Origen, therefore, every soul (except that of Christ) is a sinful soul before it ever enters upon the sphere of existence in this world. Sin is the very cause of there being any world of becoming at all.

But these speculations had no prospect of any general acceptance in the Church. The majority followed St Paul in looking not to some pre-cosmic fall but to the sin of Adam as the reason for the hold of mortality on human life. If they accepted Paul's teaching that death entered into the world by sin, they accepted his teaching also that sin entered into the world by one man, Adam (Rom. 5. 12). Through Adam's sin man lost those supernatural graces with which God in his generosity had originally endowed him, he lost that potentiality of growth into immortality which had been God's original intention for him. In their place he received a corruption of nature, an innate tendency to sin. It was not that all future generations of men were responsible for Adam's sin—how could they be, when they were not even born? But being of the same nature as Adam, they could not remain unaffected by what had happened to him. The materialistically-minded Tertullian, with the unusual Stoic background to his thought, regarded the soul (as he did God) as a very refined form of matter, and believed therefore that it was literally transmitted in tainted form from generation to generation. But in this he is as unrepresentative of the main body of thought as are the speculations of Origen. The general view was simply that through Adam mankind had contracted the malady of sin. Their freedom of choice, their capacity to do right, had not been totally removed. But in practice the dice were loaded inescapably against them. They had the disease and sooner or later it would show itself in sins of their own wilful choosing. Sin was universal; and because sin was universal, so also was death.

The Western church always took a more pessimistic view of human nature than the East. Nor was she so strongly convinced of the inviolable nature of human freedom. So at this point, and particularly in the person of Augustine, the West went further than the East in the account that it gave of the hold of sin on human life. It is not only that Augustine holds a very strong view of the nature of the taint of sin and the way in which it inevitably expresses itself in actual sins on the part of every man. He brought also into the picture two further ideas which have exercised a great and baneful influence on the later mind of the Western church.

In the first place Augustine develops his own account of the means by which the effects of Adam's sin are transmitted from generation to generation. Adam's sin had consisted essentially in a rebellion against his rightful position of dependence on God and a perverted preference for lesser goods. This, in Augustine's language, is concupiscence and it is the essence of sin. Like the influence of mortality in the thought of Theodore whereby man is unable to think or to choose in the true perspective of eternity, so concupiscence is the wrongful desire for lesser temporal pleasures. One of the most potent forms of such lesser pleasures—and one of particular significance in Augustine's own experience—was desire for the pleasures of sex and of marriage. Augustine did not regard sexual intercourse itself as evil, but he did regard the sexual excitement which accompanies it to be a result of the fall. Thus concupiscence, in this specialised sense of sexual excitement, was present in every act of intercourse. Augustine, as a Platonist, could not share Tertullian's view that a tainted soul-substance was passed on in every human birth. But since concupiscence, the essence of Adam's sin, was in at the birth, or more strictly at the conception, of every child, it seemed natural to suppose that it was the medium through which that taint was passed on.

But more significant still was the fact that Augustine was not content to stop in his thinking at the point of an inherited taint. Apart from hints in some of his immediate predecessors in the West, the Church had always stopped short at that point. Guilt was only conceivable where there was a responsible agent. The generations unborn could not have been guilty of Adam's sin for the simple reason that they were not there. Or was there a sense in which they were there? The Bible speaks of Levi paying tithes in Abraham because as his descendant he was already in some sense present in the loins of his ancestor (Heb. 7. 9). In that sense all men were present in the loins of Adam. If Levi can be said to pay tithes in Abraham, then all men can be said to sin in Adam. And had not Paul explicitly said just that? Romans 5. 12 speaks of death passing to all men "for that all have sinned". That is the only possible rendering of the original Greek text. But Augustine read his Bible in Latin. And the Latin version could be read to mean what still stands in our A.V. margin—"in whom all have sinned". So, in Augustine's eyes, Paul had directly stated that all men sinned in Adam. The whole of mankind had been present in the voluntary agent, Adam, as he freely willed his sinful act. The whole of mankind, therefore, before ever committing any separate sins of their own, before even entering the world, were guilty sinners and as such were under just sentence of death.

There was thus considerable variety concerning both the extent and the manner in which the hold of sin over human life was envisaged. But about the basic fact there was no difference of opinion. All men sin and are responsible for their sinning. Sin is a universal problem, it is the fundamental problem of the human state. How then was the Christian message of salvation understood as an answer to the need of man as sinner?

The outstanding feature in the thought of the great majority of the writings of the Fathers is that atonement, the dealing with the problem of man's sin, is regarded not so much as something done to God but rather as something done by God. But if atonement be seen as an act whose direction is from rather than towards God, the question naturally arises: What then is the direction of the act of atonement? To what or to whom is it directed? And the main answer to that question is Satan. The dealing with man's sin is an act of God directed against the devil. We shall never understand the thought of the Fathers about human sin and God's remedy for it unless we recognise the very real hold which the personalised powers of evil were felt to have in every department of human life. The powers of sin and of death were the personal power of Satan over man. How then was this power broken?

We have already seen the importance which the fifth chapter of Paul's Epistle to the Romans had for the Fathers in their thinking about the way in which sin and death had come to exercise their sway over man. It was of almost equal importance in guiding their ideas about God's answer. That is only as it should have been, for God's answer to sin was Paul's chief concern in that section of his epistle. Paul was not primarily interested in speculation about the origins of sin, he was primarily interested in making clear the nature of Christ's saving work. His discussion of Adam's sin is undertaken not for its own sake, but that by contrast it may throw light on Christ's salvation. This theme is taken up and vividly developed by Irenaeus. The first Adam, God's virgin creation, was, through the agency of a woman, overcome by Satan at the tree of disobedience and so fell into Satan's power. The second Adam, virgin-born from a woman of a different calibre, overcame Satan by his victory over temptation and by his obedience at the tree of crucifixion. So Satan's power was broken. Jesus had spoken of the stronger than the strong, who binds the strong man, enters his house and plunders his goods (Luke 11. 21–2). That was what Christ was doing throughout his ministry. It was what he did supremely in his death. In his death Christ enters into the innermost recesses of the strong man's house and there finds his plunder—namely man, whom the devil had first deceived into disobedience and ever after held firmly in his sway. It was important to Irenaeus that this second Adam, whose obedience undoes the disobedience of the first Adam, should be man as the first had been. But it was just as important that he should be God. For only God was stronger than the strong; only God could conquer in the struggle with Satan and wrest his prey from him.

This picture of a divine victory in combat over Satan provides the ground-plan for the Fathers' thinking about the atonement. It is the frame in which most of their speculation is set. But its weakness (or perhaps one should say its strength) is that it does not really explain anything. It simply tells the story of the cross and resurrection in the vigorous, picturesque language of an epic struggle between God and the devil. It does little to show how that death and resurrection dealt not only with the problem of mortality but also with the prior problem of sin that lies behind it. It was inevitable that the Fathers, while accepting and freely using this outline picture, should seek to penetrate further into the question of what it means to say that Christ died for our sins. Moreover the Bible uses many other images besides that of conquest when it speaks of the meaning of the death of Christ. These also the Fathers used freely, though never attempting the impossible task of integrating them all into one full and coherent explanation.

One such image that did lend itself to development within the framework of what has been called a "*Christus victor*" theory of the atonement was the description of Christ's death as a "ransom for many" (Mark 10. 45). If atonement be an act of God directed towards the devil, then was the ransom price a price that was paid by God and was it to the devil that he paid it? The Fathers felt the embarrassment of the question, but for the majority of them the answer to the question had to be "Yes". Because of their sin the hold that the devil had over men was a just one. If he were to release sinful man from his sway, he had a right to compensation, a right that a just God must acknowledge. What then was the ransom that was paid? Nothing less than the human soul of Christ. Over that, since it was free from sin, the devil had no rights. But it was a prize of greater value than all the other souls of men; in exchange for that one he would gladly give up all the rest. But in the end the devil was not able even to keep his ransom price. Like Shylock he had not realised the full implication of the bargain into which he had entered. He did not recognise the divinity veiled by its union with Christ's human nature. As Gregory of Nyssa puts it in a striking if unattractive image: "The hook of divinity was gulped down along with the bait of flesh." The divinity having thus found surreptitious entry into the devil's domain of death burst open the prison doors for ever by his resurrection from the dead.

It is not difficult to sympathise with those of the Fathers, like Gregory of Nyssa's friend the other Gregory of Nazianzus, who will have no truck with any such explanation, who dismiss the idea of God paying a ransom to the tyrant Satan as an impossible blasphemy. But we need also to recognise what it was that led men of such intelligence as Gregory of Nyssa to develop so apparently preposterous a theory. The idea of a struggle between God and the powers of evil is, as we have seen, not one that by itself is capable of precise or rigorous exposition. If one attempts to treat it in that way, then something like Gregory of Nyssa's theory is liable to emerge. The struggle changes into a business transaction or a law-suit, images where greater precision of thought is possible but which for all that are far less satisfactory images—especially when God's part in the transaction or the law-suit is one that bears all the marks of sharp practice. Certainly Gregory's account is one that goes far beyond what the mind of the Church as a whole would accept. But bizarre though the detail may be, the aim and direction of his account are true to what the Church wanted to say. Atonement was an act of God, an act alike of justice and of power in which the effects of man's sin were dealt with decisively. Christ's human nature was a necessary element in the achievement of that goal, but the effective power in the action belonged to his divine nature. It was through and through a work of God.

Other images used by the Bible about the death of Christ fit even less easily into a general understanding of the atonement as an act of God. They were not for that reason totally neglected by the Fathers. Athanasius, as we have seen, spoke of Christ's death as the paying of a debt to meet the just claims of God's law. Origen, whose sermons often took the form of Christian interpretation of the Old Testament law books, speaks of Christ's death as a sacrifice propitiating the Father and reconciling him to man. Such pictures suggest an understanding of the atonement as an act directed to God rather than an act initiated and effected by him. Nonetheless even when they develop images of this kind the Fathers do so, at whatever cost of inconsistency in detailed reasoning, in a way that presents them not simply as acts directed towards God but still also as acts of God. If it is God's law that has to be met, it is also God who meets it. If it is God who has to be reconciled, it is God also who is the reconciler. The atonement is not to be thought of as an act of human initiative. It is a divine act into which the human nature of Christ has been taken and in which it has its role to play. But in essence it is an act of God alike in its initiation and in its execution.

Salvation from sin, difficult and varied though its

detailed explication might have to be, had undoubtedly been secured for man by the unique and decisive act of God in Christ. But the fruits of that saving act had still to be received into the lives of men if it was to have its proper and intended effect. At the level of overcoming the bare fact of man's mortality, the incarnation and resurrection could be thought of as universal and automatic in their working. It was human nature in its entirety that had received an injection of divinity by the fact of the incarnation; it was humanity as a whole that had been brought through death by the resurrection of Christ. Sinner and saint alike must have an immortal resurrection body so that, in St Paul's words, they might "receive the things done in their bodies" (2 Cor. 5. 10). But at the level of salvation from sin, at the level of receiving the eternal blessedness of the heavenly kingdom, no such universal or automatic working was ever taught. Here there was need of an explicit, chosen response of man. Even Origen, one of the very few of the Fathers to believe that all men would ultimately be saved, believed that this would come about not by some compelling fiat of the divine will but by man's freely chosen response to the love of God in the course of those infinite ages through which the divine mercy would continue to plead. The prison doors might be open in virtue of Christ's divine redemptive act. But men had still to choose to get up and come out of the prison. That was man's part.

For the majority of the Fathers this raised no great or insuperable problem. They knew themselves to be accredited to teach a gospel of the grace of God. This was the task they believed themselves to be fulfilling. If a man came to a saving faith in God, was this not evidently the outcome of the working of God's grace? The initial, objective saving act of Christ, the preaching of the word calling forth the response of faith, even the endowment of man with freedom of the will which makes a response of faith a meaningful possibility—all these were evidence of the prior working of the grace of God to which the man who responds has contributed nothing. The response of faith alone was man's part. It might be only a very small thing, no greater than a grain of mustard seed. But it at least must be man's part. For if everything were the work of God, would not all men be in a state of faith and of salvation? Man had indeed contracted the malady of sin, but not in a way that obliterated his freedom of choice altogether. Sinner though he was, an initial minimal response of faith was surely not beyond his power.

But as with sin, so with the grace that meets man's sin, Augustine was not content to stop at the point where all his predecessors in the Church had been content to stop. If we say that the issue of a man's salvation or damnation hinges on his response of faith, and that the initiation of that faith, however small, lies in the man's own power, then do we not after all give the vital role in man's salvation to man himself and not to God?

At first Augustine was prepared to answer his question in terms that remained within the Church's traditional understanding of the working of God's grace. If grace remains outside of us, Augustine argues, if it consists only of what Christ has done in the historic past, of what the preached word tells us, of what God did for us in our initial creation, then grace fails to meet us at the point of our greatest need. For it is just here, in our responding to the good when it is shown to us, that we are most weak. Concupiscence, which is the essence of man's sin, is precisely this, too strong a love of lesser things and too weak a love of God. Man's deepest need is that he does not love the good strongly enough truly to will it and to seek it. If faith involves the willing of God's will, it cannot be wholly ours. But nor can it be wholly God's. For faith is the consent by which we accept God's gifts. Logic itself requires that such an act of accepting must be ours. Faith therefore is neither wholly God's nor wholly ours. It is both. In the act of faith there is a mysterious union of the divine and the human which cannot be torn in two.

But towards the end of his life Augustine goes further in his determination to do justice to the absolute priority of the grace of God. In doing so he goes beyond what the mind of the Church as a whole had wanted to say; he also goes beyond what most of his successors in the Church today would wish to say. The logic of his arguments for the priority of the divine eventually outweighed the reservations which he himself had earlier felt and cogently expressed, until in the end he can write: "Even our willing is effected apart from us." Was this not what Paul himself had taught? When Paul asked the rhetorical question, "What hast thou that thou hast not received?" (1 Cor. 7. 25), must not faith be understood to be one of those things which man has received? Indeed was not the same truth taught more explicitly still by the same Paul when he wrote: "He has mercy on whom he will have mercy, and whom he will he hardens" (Rom. 9. 18). Greek interpreters had argued that the words referred only to God's foreknowledge and did nothing to destroy man's freedom. Theodore of Mopsuestia had even attempted the impossible feat of treating them not as Paul's positive affirmation but as words of an imaginary objector whom Paul quotes only in order to refute. But there is no denying that in their plain sense the words are strong support for Augustine's case. If the objection to ascribing even the response of faith to God had been that no reason then was left why some had faith and some did not, why all were not saved, here was the answer. God chose some to be recipients of his mercy and not others. If this appears to us to be injustice, we must recall that if justice be our plea all without exception would suffer eternal condemnation for their guilt in Adam's sin. If we still protest the unfairness of selecting only some to be the recipients of grace, we will be told that the answer to our question lies hidden in the inscrutable mystery of the divine will. Mystery there must be somewhere. But it is hard not to feel that the mystery of God's inscrutable predestinating will, to which Augustine appeals in his later years, is a less satisfactory statement of the real mystery of Christian faith than that of the interaction of divine grace and human freedom in the experience of willing and of faith, which he had emphasised at an earlier stage of his career.

Summary

There is no equivalent to the Athanasian creed or the Chalcedonian Definition, which gives a formal statement of the Church's teaching about man's sin and God's salvation. For that we may be grateful. Man's need and its remedy is too varied a thing to lend itself satisfactorily to such systematised treatment. Formalised accounts cannot avoid the kind of over-simplification that leads to serious distortion. The teaching of the Fathers on this theme has its faults, but its unsystematic character and its many-sidedness are not to be classed among them.

The teaching that we have surveyed is a curious mixture of profound insights and preposterous theorising. The ruling idea of the atonement as a divine victory over the powers of evil is a vision of great power, whose value is not dependent on such devious developments as the idea of the deception of the devil. Augustine's understanding of man's need is one of great psychological and spiritual insight. Man is not an island; he does not start even his life, let alone each day, with a blank sheet, with a completely open possibility for good or evil. We are bound together through heredity and environment in a corporate existence where evil as well as good is operative. Our deepest need is not wise counsel, not even forgiveness of the past, but the transformation of our inner beings at their deepest roots. And those Christians who have shown the fullest evidence of such transformation have been the most sure that it was not of their own doing. But when the same Augustine externalises and rationalises those insights in terms of an original guilt handed on through the presence of concupiscence in the act of intercourse and of a divine predestination whose justice is hidden in the inscrutable will of God, then we are being offered an account which the Christian conscience can only reject with all the force at its command.

Traditionally the main objection that has been brought against the Fathers' approach to the theme of salvation has been their treatment of the subject in terms of natures, in terms of a change imparted to human nature as a whole by that divine nature with which it was indissolubly linked at the incarnation. Certainly it is not an approach which many people are likely to want to adopt as their own at the present time. But just because it is an approach that is not immediately congenial to us today, it is the more important that we resist the temptation to make a caricature of it. It never amounted to treating salvation as something magical or automatic. It was never intended to minimise the essentially personal nature of God's act or of man's response. Rather it was designed to emphasise that the personal activity of God in the work of salvation could not be fully expressed in individualistic terms, but must be understood also in corporate and in cosmic terms. If we undertake to express for ourselves the truth of God's salvation in more directly personal ways (as we should), we need to beware lest it is we who fall short in presenting it in too exclusively individualistic a manner. We do not find it easy to do justice to the social and the cosmic aspects of experience in a genuinely personal way, but that is not to say that they do not need to be seen as very real dimensions of experience to which the saving work of Christ is of direct and lasting relevance.

Chapter Five

THE SACRAMENTS

SALVATION has to be received; it has to be made real and effective in the ordinary lives of men and women. The most expressive means of that reception in Christian practice is the sacraments. The very meaning of baptism is the initial acceptance of the salvation won by Christ; the very meaning of the eucharist is the continually renewed acceptance of that same salvation in daily life. The physical character of sacraments means that they are particularly vulnerable to the charge of implying an idea of God's salvation as something made available to man in a magical or automatic way. This is not a necessary concomitant of sacramental practice, though it is a real danger against which the sacramentalist has always to be on his guard. It is therefore not surprising that critics who are already suspicious of the idea of a transformation of natures, which is so prominent a feature of the teaching of the Fathers, should be made more uneasy still when they read of that transformation being made effective by sacramental means. Nowhere is it more important to approach the teaching of the Fathers in the light of their presuppositions and not of ours. Their understanding of symbols is far more positive, far more realistic than ours. For them it is natural to think of the symbol as in some way embodying the reality which it expresses; it is the positive relation of the symbol to that reality rather than the distinction between them which is paramount. This makes it natural for them to speak in strongly realistic terms of the outward sacramental forms. If we simply attend to their language and ask what the same words would mean on our lips, we shall misunderstand what they were intending to say and what they have still of value to say to us.

The physical nature of the sacraments was a matter of especial importance to those early writers, like Irenaeus, whose primary concern was the refutation of Gnosticism. Most Gnostics had their sacramental rituals. But the orthodox insisted on their inconsistency in so doing. How could the evil material stuff of this world be used to embody the means of man's salvation from it? It would be a case of casting out devils through Beelzebub, the prince of devils. Sacramental practice necessarily implies a positive attitude to the material world and its potentiality for use within the purposes of God. The attitude of the early Fathers to the physical aspect of the sacraments was therefore strongly positive. A sacrament, of course, was always more than its outward form, but that outward form was a very important part of it.

Water, the material element in baptism, has a universal significance in the life of men. Coming down as rain on the earth, it is essential to the existence of life in any form. It is everywhere used for the purpose of cleansing and purifying, alike of men and metals. It is no arbitrary sign but one perfectly suited to the high office which God has assigned to it, and the Fathers were keen to emphasise that fact. Most subtly of all, Gregory of Nyssa argues that since a very small drop of water in the form of the male seed can effect the miracle of human birth it is wholly appropriate that water should be the effective medium in bringing about man's spiritual rebirth.

More commonly still the role played by water in baptism is linked with the role played by water at earlier stages in the divine plan as recorded in the Scriptures. It was the Spirit of God moving on the face of the waters which had been the operative power in the initial work of creation

(Gen. 1. 2); it was appropriate that the same association of water and Spirit should be the operative agents in the work of God's new creation. Noah was saved from destruction by the wood of the ark floating on the waters of the flood; so man now is saved from judgment and death by the wood of the cross and the waters of baptism. Israel was finally rescued from the power of the Egyptians by the waters of the Red Sea; so the Christian passes to safety through the waters of baptism while the evil powers which formerly held him in bondage are overwhelmed and drowned there. The detailed parallels sound forced and strange to our ears. So no doubt they are; and they become even more so when one writer insists that every single reference to water in the whole of Scripture is really a hidden reference to baptism. But they have firm roots in Scripture. 1 Peter 3. 20 had likened the flood to baptism and 1 Corinthians 10. 2 the Red Sea. Taken as a whole, such imagery helped the Christian to see the salvation which he received in baptism as standing in continuity with the creative and saving work of God right through the ages.

But the rite of baptism as a whole has an even richer symbolism than that which can be provided by the element of water considered by itself. St Paul had spoken in Romans 6 of baptism in terms of being buried with Christ and raised again with him. This understanding of the rite was strongly reinforced both by its form and its occasion. The normal form of baptism was a baptism of adults by triple immersion. The going under the water and coming up again from under it was a vivid picture of burial and resurrection. The fact that it was done three times was primarily associated with the threefold name of Father, Son and Holy Spirit; but even that detail could also suggest the three days of Christ's sojourn in the grave. Moreover the rite was normally administered with great solemnity once a year on the night between Holy Saturday and Easter Sunday morning. Everything about it spoke eloquently of death and resurrection. In the Eastern Church in particular this understanding of it was fully and richly developed.

Those who were to be baptised underwent a long period of catechumenate. The climax of this period of preparation in the fourth century was a thorough course of instruction throughout the period of Lent. We have a record of the catechetical lectures delivered by Cyril of Jerusalem about the year 350. In one of the last of these, delivered in Easter week itself, Cyril recalls for his hearers, now newly baptised, the meaning of the rite which they have just undergone. Christ, he says, was stripped, crucified, buried and rose again; all this was done in reality. They in their baptism have imitated what Christ did. They too stripped off their tunics, were buried beneath the waters and rose again out of them. What happened to them admittedly was not the reality that Christ's act was. Theirs was an imitation, an image of his. But the salvation that it brought them was fully real.

Gregory of Nyssa, always keen to give an explanation of why things are what they are, insists on the appropriateness of receiving our salvation through imitative acts. The man who is lost in a maze must follow precisely the footsteps of his would-be saviour. Christ saved us by what he did; we receive that salvation by our imitative acts. This sounds like imitative magic. But it is not. Christ's acts are saving acts because they embody and express what he is. Our imitative acts have saving power for us, only if they embody and express what we are. In his first introductory lecture to his would-be catechumens Cyril had reminded them of the story of Simon Magus and the uselessness of baptism where the heart is not right (Acts 8. 13–24). When the Fathers speak of the saving power of baptism, it is never the bare rite that they mean; it is baptism and faith together as an inseparable unity which they intend.

These ideas about the meaning of baptism belonged to the whole Church, but they were not at first developed with the same depth of insight in the West as in the East. Western writers seldom penetrate as deeply into the inner heart of things as their Eastern counterparts. They tend to be more concerned with matters of practice, and are inclined to remain content with a more obvious, if also more superficial, account of the meaning of their faith. So it was in the case of baptism. It was an issue of major importance to early Western writers, but their interest arises more out of particular practical problems and their understanding of the sacrament is usually couched in more straightforward but less profound categories. Three problems of this kind are of particular importance.

1. *Baptism and the Laying on of Hands*

It is St Paul who describes baptism as burial with Christ and resurrection with him. The other main interpretation of baptism in the New Testament is to be found in the writings of St John. He speaks of the need for a man to "be born of water and of Spirit" (John 3. 5). This concentrates attention on the picture of baptism as a rebirth brought about by the joint agency of two factors, the outward element of water and the accompanying power of the Spirit. This picture lies behind much early Western thought. The materialistically-minded Tertullian suggests that as the Spirit hovered over the waters at the first creation, so the Spirit now hovers over the waters of baptism and actually imparts to them something of his holiness. But the idea is not typical of the main thought of the Church. The normal picture is the more obvious one. Where the outward element of water is rightly used, there the inward power of the Spirit is at work.

But the Spirit is more than just the agent by whom God's gifts are given. He is himself the sum and essence of those gifts. For if baptism be the moment of man's acceptance of God's salvation, he receives not only illumination, rebirth and remission of sin; he receives the Spirit himself. If in baptism a man is made Christ's, then in baptism a man must receive the Spirit; the idea of a Christian without the Spirit is a contradiction in terms. "If any man have not the Spirit of Christ, he is none of his" (Rom. 8. 9). The majority of early Christian writers, following St Paul, see this whole complex of ideas as a unity. Baptism and the giving of the Spirit must belong together.

But there was another influence pointing in a different direction. Chapter 8 of the book of Acts gives a detailed account of the conversion of some Samaritans as a result of the preaching of Philip. They are baptised by Philip, but do not receive the Spirit. Peter and John lay hands on them, and they do receive the Spirit. In the earliest liturgical practice known to us (about the end of the second century) the baptism in water is followed both by an anointing with oil and a laying on of hands. It was natural for the giving of the Spirit to be associated especially with the action of the laying on of hands. Thus Tertullian can write in general terms of man receiving the Spirit in baptism, but then corrects himself and speaking with more precision says: "Not that in the waters we receive the Holy Spirit, but in the water we are cleansed and prepared for the Holy Spirit." He then goes on to link the gift of the Spirit explicitly with the laying on of hands.

As long as these were regarded as two parts of a single rite (as clearly they were by Tertullian) no great difficulty arises. But let the two once become separated and a severe tension was bound to arise. The clearest signs we have of this beginning to happen are in the Church of Rome during the third century. There was more than one cause. There was the question of those who had received emergency baptism, which did not include the laying on of hands, when thought to be dying but who subsequently recovered. Similar emergencies could arise in times of persecution. Again the Roman Church accepted the validity of baptisms performed by schismatic groups, which had broken away from the main body of the Church. She did not require those who wished to enter the Church from such bodies to be baptised all over again; but she did require them to receive a laying on of hands through which they would receive the Holy Spirit. Man, St John had said, must be born of water and of the Spirit. Man, this appeared to imply, must receive both water-baptism and the laying on of hands. Both sacraments, it was said, are necessary. It was a natural development of ideas, but a disastrous one. From any such division of spheres of influence water-baptism must inevitably come off badly. All that is left to it is to be, in Tertullian's words, a preparatory cleansing. The rich, positive values of salvation all cohere in the laying on of hands. But it was baptism of which the New Testament spoke so forcefully; it was the ritual in the water which expressed so profoundly man's death and resurrection with Christ. Whatever the logic of the situation, it was impossible for baptism to be turned into nothing more than a secondary, preparatory rite.

In practice water-baptism and the laying on of hands continued in normal circumstances to go together in a single rite, as they do to this day in the Eastern Church even with the practice of infant baptism. But they could, if need be, be separated. At times they were, and in the West those times grew more frequent as the centuries went by. Where they were separate, it was natural to try also to split up the meaning of the rite also into two separate parts. But there was no satisfactory way in which it could be done. If emergency baptism with water only made a man in any sense a Christian, it made no sense to deny that the Spirit was given there. But the laying on of hands was particularly linked with that very thing in both Scripture and tradition. Countless attempts were made in succeeding centuries to divide up the giving of the Spirit itself into two halves— an initial and a confirmatory giving, a coming in regeneration and a coming in seven-fold power. But for the most part the Fathers were content to associate the giving of the Spirit indiscriminately with baptism or with the laying on of hands, even where this appeared to lead them into inconsistencies in what they believed and taught.

2. *Post-Baptismal Sin*

The simplest of all pictures of baptism is that of baptism as a washing. In the baptismal bath the mire of past evil is washed away; all old sins are forgiven. But the picture clearly suggests that the efficacy of baptism is purely retrospective in character. Indeed, it was felt, could it with relation to the root problem of sin be otherwise? Must it not be so, if baptism were to be more than a magical charm? Past sins were forgiven; the keeping power of the Holy Spirit was made available; the path to good works and ultimate fellowship with God lay wide open. But man was still free; man had still to tread that path for himself. Baptism was no automatic passport to heavenly bliss whatever a man might do after it even to the point of abjuring his faith. What had been gained in baptism could be lost again. Baptism represented a real change in man's status with God, but it was not an irrevocable change.

When baptism is viewed in these terms as a new start, as a wiping clean of the slate, there arises inevitably the problem of serious post-baptismal sin. There is a clear strand of teaching in the later writings of the New Testament which teaches that for such sin there is no possibility of forgiveness. Nothing can be done for the dog who returns to his own vomit, for the sow that was washed and returns to her wallowing in the mire (2 Pet. 2. 20–22, cf. Heb. 6.

4–6; 1 John 5. 16). Like Esau he has had his opportunity and deliberately thrown it away; no further chance can be given him though he seek it carefully with tears (Heb. 12. 16–17). This was the general view of the second-century Church. "There is no repentance save that which took place when we went down into the waters and received remission of our former sins."

Only the harshest of puritans, only the most insensitive reader of the gospels could remain indefinitely satisfied with such a creed. Once again it is in Rome, second-century Rome, that the pressure was most strongly felt. The prophet Hermas (c. A.D. 140) was acutely aware of the pastoral problem of lapsed Christians. Like a naïve reformer he declared that God was giving to the Church a single, unrepeatable opportunity for a second repentance. Those who had fallen by the wayside could be gathered in and then the Church would resume her old pattern of allowing only the one forgiveness at a man's baptism. But such a call was no solution; it could be no more than a brief postponement of the problem.

If baptism was unrepeatable and dealt only with past sins, what was to be done? One could play safe and postpone one's baptism until one's deathbed. It was done not infrequently. But it made no sense. Baptism could no more be turned into a rite for the dying, thereby making the living Church a church of catechumens, than it could be turned into a curtain-raiser for the laying on of hands. The outcome was inevitable. Some other means must be found for dealing with sin after baptism. Good works, almsgiving, but above all penance duly administered by the Church, were all taught to have propitiatory effect, dealing with those later sins with which baptism was no longer able to deal. So once again there grew up out of the problems of baptismal practice another sacrament, the sacrament of penance. There is an air of inevitability about the whole process of development. But the introduction of such secondary, subsidiary ways of forgiveness could not help but detract from a full appreciation of the real meaning of baptism. Baptism was the means of receiving the benefits of the salvation won by Christ. The need for other ways of forgiveness to meet sins for which baptism could not avail seemed to suggest that that salvation was not as complete a work as Christian preaching would have us believe.

3. *Infant Baptism*

The origins of the practice of infant baptism are a matter of fierce debate at the present time. There are some who believe it goes back to the time of the New Testament itself, which certainly speaks of the baptism of whole households. But there is no explicit reference to the practice before the close of the second century. Certainly by the middle of the third century the custom was widely established, and it quickly came to be regarded (whether rightly or wrongly) as a tradition that had come down from apostolic times. What led to its adoption? We have virtually no evidence from which to judge—indeed the lack of any sign of debates about the issue is one of the arguments used by those who believe that the practice must have gone back to the very beginnings of Christian history. It seems unlikely that ideas about inherited sin played a major role in its adoption. Tertullian believed in an "antecedent evil in the soul which arises from its corrupt origin", but he was still more impressed by the problem of post-baptismal sin. The reception of baptism, he argues, is more to be feared than its delay; was it not dangerous for the young to be rushed into baptism before they had sown their wild oats? Thus the thought of the man who held to the idea of the soul's inherited taint more strongly than any other early thinker is weighted as a whole against the practice. We can only guess at the reasons which led to its becoming the regular practice of the Church, but the development is not really a surprising one. Baptism was the means of entry into the Christian fellowship; it was the source of those positive graces by which the Christian lives his life. Was it not natural that Christian parents should desire these things for their children, for every member of the close-knit unit of the family, from the start of their lives?

But if the causes of infant baptism be largely a matter for speculation, the outcome of its practice is not. Baptism as administered to infants was the same baptism as that given to adults. It had other aspects, but first and foremost it was baptism "for the remission of sins". Moreover, as we have seen, this was regularly understood to mean baptism for the remission of past sins. The implications are obvious. Augustine was not the first to point them out, though as so often it is he who does so with the most uncompromising rigour. Infant baptism, he believed, was a custom from apostolic times; it could not be void of meaning. It could only mean that even the new-born infant had sins to be forgiven. What could such sins be other than the infant's share in the sin of Adam? The practice therefore reinforced the ideas about inherited guilt, which we have already seen to be a natural outcome of Augustine's understanding of the character and scope of human sin. So in infant baptism it was forgiveness of the inherited guilt of Adam's sin that the child received. But Augustine's logic took him a step further. The infant who died without baptism died with that guilt still on him. For him there could be no salvation; his destination could only be hell—albeit those who had added no actual sin of their own to the sin of their inheritance would have the lightest of hell's punishments to undergo.

We may be glad that the British heretic, Pelagius (c. A.D. 410), rebelled at such teaching. But he had no clear or logical alternative to offer. For he too fully accepted the practice of infant baptism. Since the unbaptised infant had committed no sins of its own, and since he rejected all ideas of inherited guilt, Pelagius could deny that it was destined for the punishments of hell without difficulty. But it was also baptism which conveyed the positive gifts of divine sonship and of entry into the Kingdom of Heaven. All this therefore the infant who died unbaptised must miss. We could not know his fate; we could only know that it was neither among the blessed in the full presence of God nor among the damned in the torments of hell. But the puzzle remains. Baptism, the one and only ground of the full and free forgiveness of man's sins, was now regularly administered to the one section of the community who had no sins to be forgiven.

Sign and meaning

These practical problems are still with us—baptism and confirmation, baptism and church discipline, and above all infant baptism. The Fathers cannot answer our problems for us, for they found no satisfactory answers for themselves. But something can be learnt from seeing the way in which the problems arose for them. Baptism and the laying on of hands will never make theological sense unless they be seen as two parts of the single rite from which they sprang. If we think of baptism as dealing only with the past, instead of as establishing a new relationship between man and God which transcends the categories of time, we shall fail to do justice to the richness of its meaning. And if we try to pour into infant baptism the full meaning of the original rite as used for adults, we raise for ourselves difficulties which have no logical solution.

But behind these particular problems lies a problem of a still more fundamental nature. Sign and meaning belong together; it is the unity of baptism and faith with which the

Fathers are primarily concerned. But in practice the two do not always go together. It is this fact which lies at the root of so many of the problems we encounter in trying to think clearly about the sacraments. The Fathers never made the mistake of putting the whole weight of the positive meaning of the sacraments on the outward form alone. Baptism by itself could not save; it was not magic. But though they never regarded the outward form as by itself sufficient, they were tempted to regard it as absolutely necessary. Salvation was not to be secured by baptism alone, but nor could it be secured without it. The catechumen who was put to death for his faith was, it is true, universally regarded as though he had been baptised. His martyrdom is his baptism, a baptism in blood. More occasionally it is claimed that the desire for baptism, which is forestalled by death even though it be not a martyr's death, may be regarded as equivalent to baptism itself. But these are very partial exceptions, and do little to mitigate the general truth of the absolute necessity of baptism.

The problem is a real one. We cannot pretend that sign and meaning always go together. That would be to live in a world of fantasy. We know that in fact they are often separated from one another. And so we are tempted to try to give an account of them in their separation. But that way lies disaster. For our account of the sacramental sign becomes then a description either of an empty shell or of a potent piece of magic. The account that we give of a sacrament must always be an account of it in its unity of sign and meaning. In practice that unity may seldom be achieved; but it is only in the light of that unity that the meaning of any particular sacramental occasion can be understood. A vase may exist in fragments. But you will never understand them by trying to understand the fragments in isolation. You can only understand them by

devoting your attention and your description to the wholeness of the now broken vase.

Eucharist and Agape

Baptism is the receiving of the fruit of Christ's saving
work through an imitation in action of the redemptive
acts of Christ himself. Such an understanding of the reception fits most naturally with an understanding of the
saviour as our forerunner, the individual pioneer, who has
gone ahead of us and now shows us the path to follow. That
was the kind of picture of Christ which was typical of the
Antiochene school. And baptism plays a role of especial
importance in the thought of the Antiochenes. But it was
not, as we have seen, the main way in which the early
Church understood Christ's saving work. For the Alexandrians in particular he was not so much the individual
pioneer as the representative God-man, the one who by
his very being made possible the divinisation of human
nature. For those who thought in such terms the eucharist
was a still more expressive sacrament than that of baptism.
For the act of eating seemed to depict a closer association,
a more intimate measure of union than the imitative
ritual of baptism.

When in the very earliest days of the Church's life
Christians met for the "breaking of bread", they met for a
common meal. The sharing of food in the ancient world
was never a purely secular occasion in the modern sense of
that word. It was a natural occasion of religious thanksgiving and of renewed fellowship between those who took
part. For the early Christian community their meals had
received new and special meaning from the life of Jesus.
They looked back not only to the Last Supper but also to
other occasions of special meals which Jesus had had with
his disciples, particularly those which he had had with
them after his resurrection. The meals spoke to them there-

123

fore not only of the broken body and the sacrifice of the cross, which had been the central theme of the Last Supper. They were natural occasions also for thanksgiving (the literal meaning of the word "eucharist") to God for all the gifts of creation, for realising the presence of the risen Christ as host at the meal, for real fellowship and sharing of common needs among themselves. But the full meal and the solemn aspect of the remembrance of Christ's sacrificial death did not always go easily together. The eleventh chapter of 1 Corinthians shows the incongruities and the improprieties that could too easily arise. The practical difficulties also as the communities grew in size must have been considerable. Detailed evidence is lacking, but it is clear that by the end of the first century eucharist and full meal were being separated from one another. The practice of community meals did not simply die out; it lived on until the seventh or eighth century. The name used for them was "agape" or love-feast. They were a kind of parish supper, often given by one of the richer members of the congregation. They were of course still religious occasions, still a part of the Church's life, but not with the same depth or solemnity of meaning. The central thing was the eucharist, which now took the form of a purely token meal.

Some aspects of the meaning of the rite belong more naturally to the joyous occasion of a full meal. General thanksgiving for God's bounty, a sense of the presiding presence of the risen Christ, the experience of fellowship and sharing within the congregation—all these arise more naturally and spontaneously in the context of a full meal. With the separating off of the "agape" as a distinct occasion, the awareness of these things within eucharistic worship was inevitably weakened. They were of course not obliterated, not wholly ignored. Indeed they are far more prominent in the eucharistic worship of the age of the

Fathers than they have been in the worship of the Western church, Catholic or Protestant, almost ever since. Nevertheless weakening there was. But on the positive side that weakening allowed the other aspects of the service to stand out in clearer focus. The eucharist was above all the feast of the body and blood of Christ and the memorial of his sacrificial death. These were the two primary ways in which the meaning of the rite was understood.

1. *Spiritual Food*

"Whoso eateth my flesh and drinketh my blood hath eternal life" (John 6. 54). The body and blood of Christ are the intended food of the Christian's spiritual life. The early Fathers do not interpret St John's words exclusively of the eucharist. That interpretation was of course never excluded or denied. But the words were referred with equal freedom to the obedient assimilation of Christ's teaching or the mystical contemplation of his person. Nevertheless the imagery of the words was the imagery of the sacrament; the eucharist was regarded naturally enough as the focal occasion of receiving the spiritual food of Christ's body and blood.

"The medicine of immortality" Ignatius of Antioch (c. A.D. 110) calls it, and no phrase has done more to convince posterity that the underlying approach of the Fathers to the sacraments was at heart a magical one. Ignatius certainly writes of the eucharist in strikingly realistic terms. He inveighs against those who "do not allow that the eucharist is the flesh of our saviour, Jesus Christ". For him that is a sign that they do not really allow that Christ had real flesh at all, it is evidence that they are amongst those who denied his real humanity altogether. All that Ignatius wrote bears the stamp of the vigorous, enigmatic style of the prophet. His language, like St John's, is language which cries aloud for more careful elucidation.

125

Such further elaboration was not long in coming. Justin Martyr has left us an invaluable, if at points tantalisingly brief description of what happened at an early Christian eucharist. Two features in his account serve to throw some light on what it meant for him to speak of the bread and the wine received in the service as spiritual food, as the flesh and blood of Christ. In the first place he speaks of a change occurring to the bread and wine which is associated with the prayers said during the course of the service. Secondly that change is to be understood in the light of the incarnation, when the Word was himself made flesh. This parallel with the incarnation was much more than just a convenient analogy. The essential meaning of the service was the receiving of Christ and of the benefits which he had won for man by his incarnation. It was naturally fitting therefore that the two, the initiating ground and the continuing means of man's salvation, should be understood in essentially similar ways. So Irenaeus declares in similar vein that when the eucharist has received the invocation of God, it is no longer common bread but consists of two realities, earthly and heavenly. Just as in the incarnation there was no question of the Word being turned into flesh, so in the eucharist there is no question of the bread and wine being turned into the body and blood of Christ. Rather, just as Jesus of Nazareth seemed to be just a man (which he was), but was in fact much more than he seemed —namely the incarnate son of God—so the eucharist is bread and wine, but also at the same time something much more than that—the body and blood of Christ.

The development of ideas about the nature of the eucharistic elements marches hand in hand with the development of ideas about the person of the incarnate Christ. It is no surprise therefore that it is in the Eastern church of the fourth century that the most notable advances are to be found. We meet there a striking conjunction of symbolic and realistic language. Cyril of Jerusalem speaks frequently of the elements as "types" or "symbols" of Christ's body and blood. But such language implies no going back on the realistic language of earlier generations. The words were never intended to imply, as they so easily can to us, that they were *only* types or *only* symbols. The symbol is also that which it symbolises. The new language is intended to give greater precision to the earlier language not to correct it. Indeed Cyril can also use the most strikingly realistic language himself. He warns his newly baptised hearers, now eligible to share in the eucharist, not to be deceived. "The apparent bread," he says, "is not bread, even though it is sensible to the touch, but the body of Christ; and the apparent wine is not wine, even though the taste will have it so, but the blood of Christ."

No systematic account of the nature of the change emerges from the period. Of its importance and of its reality there was no doubt. There was also an increasing precision in defining the moment of its occurrence. As the Word had been made flesh "by the operation of the Holy Spirit", so prayer was made to that same Holy Spirit to effect a like transformation in the case of the bread and wine. To this day in the Eastern church it is a prayer of this kind to the Holy Spirit (an "epiclesis" as it is called) which is regarded as vital for the consecration of the elements rather than as in the West the repetition of the words of institution. The way in which the different Fathers write or speak about the elements thus consecrated corresponds closely with the way they write and speak about the incarnate Christ. The Antiochenes, who insisted so strongly on the co-existence of the two natures, divine and human, in the one Christ, speak similarly of the double nature of the eucharist, at once bread and wine and body and blood. The Alexandrians, who so stressed the priority of Christ's divine nature as to seem at times to leave little place for his humanity, also speak of the eucharist in such a way that, while the continuing existence of the bread and wine is not denied, its importance is so played down, as in the words quoted from Cyril of Jerusalem, as to amount almost in practice to a denial. The thing that was important religiously was the thing that was not obvious to the senses. It is that side of the reality, therefore, on which overwhelming emphasis is laid.

The main purpose of this whole tradition of a transformation of the bread and wine into the body and blood of Christ was to assure men of a living union with Christ himself through their reception of the sacrament. "Whoso eateth my flesh and drinketh my blood hath eternal life." Men needed to know that the bread and the wine were nothing less than the body of Christ himself, imbued with all his life-giving power; and then they needed to eat and to drink, to receive it into their own being. In the incarnation the divine Word had made himself accessible to the human senses. In the eucharist he not only makes himself accessible to the outer senses; he makes himself assimilable, says Gregory of Nyssa, through eating and digestion even to the very bodies of men, so that the whole man, body and soul alike, may receive the divinising power of the Word and share his blessed immortality.

But the way in which the tradition grew up, with its particular moment of consecration, led to ideas about the body and blood of Christ being developed in other contexts as well as that of their reception as spiritual food. If the bread and wine are changed into the body and blood of Christ at the moment of consecration then they are there, present in their own right as it were, upon the altar. This way of worship was partly fostered by, and itself fostered still further, a tradition of popular devotion embodying superstitious ideas of an objective and localised presence of Christ's body. Such ideas were a significant by-product of this whole approach and should not be ignored. But they were not its main intention and should not be allowed to have the last word.

An increase of precision in sacramental definition does not necessarily mean an increase in profundity. Too often it means rather a misleading disruption of that unity of form and meaning without which a sacrament is no sacrament. Few early authors write about the eucharist with the same degree of profundity as Augustine; few are more difficult to tie down. With the most convinced realists he can say: "That bread which you can see on the altar, sanctified by the word of God, is Christ's body. That cup, or rather the contents of that cup, sanctified by the word of God, is Christ's blood." But he can also say: "Why make ready your teeth and your belly? Believe and you have eaten." In the conjunction of the two is the heart of the tradition of the Fathers. No language is too strong to make real the wonder and the completeness of that union with himself which Christ has made available to us in the eucharist. It is the medicine of immortality. But it is not magic.

2. *Sacrifice*

"From the rising of the sun even unto the going down of the same my name shall be great among the Gentiles; and in every place incense shall be offered unto my name, and a pure offering; for my name shall be great among the nations, says the Lord of hosts" (Mal. 1. 11). This prophecy of Malachi, so the Fathers believed, had been fulfilled in the spread of the Christian Church throughout the Gentile world. More particularly the pure offering of which Malachi had spoken was to be seen in the Christian eucharist now celebrated in different places all over the known world.

But what sort of an offering was it? The Old Testament

sacrifices had been brought to a final end by their fulfilment in the sacrificial death of Christ. In what sense was the eucharist a Christian sacrifice? To that question two main lines of answer were given by the earliest writers like Justin Martyr and Irenaeus.

In the first place it was emphasised that the real sacrifice is the sacrifice of the heart. Many of the most religious minds, both Gentile and Jewish, had begun to turn away with distaste from the old custom of animal sacrifice and to stress the inward, spiritual nature of all true sacrifice. "In the time to come," says one of the Rabbis, "all other sacrifices will cease, but the sacrifice of thanksgiving will never cease." With such a sentiment the Christian could heartily concur. Did not the very word "eucharist" mean "thanksgiving"? That was just what it was. It was a pure offering, a spiritual offering of thanksgiving, the proper sacrifice of the new age which Christ had inaugurated by his death and resurrection.

But the eucharist was not in fact a purely spiritual (in the sense of non-material) offering; it involved a material element as well, and one that was of great significance in the thought of the opponents of Gnosticism, like Irenaeus. And so there had to be also a second account of the way in which the eucharist was a pure offering, a way which took account of the bread and the wine which were used in the service. It was an offering of the first-fruits of creation to the creator God, who, whatever the Gnostics might say, was the God of Christian faith and worship.

So the eucharist was both a spiritual offering of thanksgiving and a material offering of bread and wine, the first-fruits of creation. But the idea of the eucharist as offering or sacrifice was bound to be related to the offering or sacrifice of the death of Christ. The thanksgiving of the eucharist was a thanksgiving above all else for Christ's sacrificial death. The bread and the wine which were offered were the same bread and wine which were transformed into the body and blood of Christ, that very body and blood which Christ had offered on the cross for the salvation of mankind. The link is first clearly and unequivocally made by Cyprian of Carthage (c. A.D. 250). We have already seen how realistically men could speak of the bread and wine as the body and blood of Christ and how such language was not always restricted to its primary context of that spiritual food which is man's nourishment for eternal life. The bread and the wine were the body and blood of Christ. And they were the material of the offering made in the eucharist. Was not the offering then plainly an offering of the body and blood of Christ? So it seemed to Cyprian. And so he writes simply and decisively: "The Lord's passion is the sacrifice we offer." It was a momentous step.

Once again for the more detailed development of this idea we must turn to the Eastern church of the succeeding century. Cyril of Jerusalem tells his new communicants that in the service "we are offering up Christ sacrificed for our sins". As in baptism there was a fruitful imitation in image of the redemptive acts of Christ, so the eucharistic service also retraces the saving events of death and resurrection. Most frequently and most naturally it is the death of Christ which is envisaged as being re-enacted in the service, and the most vividly realistic language can be used to describe it. The priest, says Gregory of Nazianzus, "draws down the Word by his word and with a bloodless cutting severs the body and blood of Christ with voice for sword". Theodore of Mopsuestia, who always thinks of mortality as man's most pressing need and the resurrection as the heart of his salvation, sees the service more in terms of the resurrection than the death of Christ. The bread and wine laid out on the white linen cloth upon the altar at the start of the service are for him the dead body of the Lord laid out for burial; with the coming down of the Spirit in

131

response to the prayer of consecration they receive the immortal life-giving character of the resurrection body of the Lord.

But there is a clear difference between the idea of the re-enactment in image of Christ's saving acts in the case of baptism and that implicit in the eucharist. In baptism there is no question of Christ going through his saving acts again even in image; it is the Christian who is the subject of those imitative acts. But in the eucharist it appears that it is Christ who retraces his own steps. It is the Word who is brought down; it is the body and blood of Christ which is severed with a bloodless cutting; it is Christ sacrificed who is offered. Is that what was really intended? Here as before it is essential to remember that symbol and reality were seen as one rather than as clearly separate. For here again symbolic and realistic language stand side by side in a single author. "We do not offer another sacrifice, as the high priests of old," says John Chrysostom, the great preacher (c. A.D. 400), "but we ever offer the same or rather we make the memorial of the sacrifice." The same sacrifice and the memorial of the sacrifice are not contrasting expressions; they are different ways of saying the same thing.

When the Fathers spoke in fully realistic terms of the bread and wine as the very body and blood of Christ, their primary purpose was to make clear that the life-giving benefits of Christ's passion were as fully available to Christians of all subsequent generations as they had been to those disciples who had shared in the Last Supper. So too when they spoke in equally realistic terms of an apparent re-enactment of the sacrifice of Calvary, they did not intend to imply that there could be a repetition of that one sacrifice; they did intend to make unmistakably clear that its propitiatory benefits were fully available in the here and now. Cyril of Jerusalem justifies the practice of intercessory prayer after the prayer of consecration by saying that "prayer offered when the most holy and awesome sacrifice is lying there is of greatest profit to the souls of those for whom the prayer is offered". Thus the sacrifice of the eucharist is linked with the sacrifice of Calvary to the point of mystical identification, and it is understood as the God-given means of bringing the fruits of that one sacrifice most effectively into the arena of contemporary life.

Once again the last word may be allowed to Augustine. It is not a word that he speaks alone, but it is a word that he speaks with particular force and clarity. No genuine offering, whether of thanksgiving or of first-fruits, can fail to be also a self-offering. Linked in to the idea of the offering of the eucharist there must always be, therefore, the idea of the Church's self-offering. She too was the body of Christ. So if she offered the body and blood of Christ in the eucharist, was she not offering herself? Indeed she was, said Augustine. On Calvary Christ had offered himself; he had been both offerer and oblation, both priest and victim. So in the eucharist the Church was offering herself. But both acts, both the offering and the being offered, were not acts that she did apart from Christ; they were acts that she did in the strength of her unity with him, as the members of his body. The offering of the eucharist was an act of that body in which Christ and the Church were one; and it was an act of self-offering, for that which was offered was the same as that which did the offering, Christ and the Church in the indissoluble unity of his mystical body.

Sacramental language is inevitably dangerous language. That which is adequate to express the vital religious purpose of the sacrament is always in danger of falling over into superstition. The line between the two is not easy to draw. There are times when the Fathers do appear to cross that line; there are many more times when those who built upon their ideas in succeeding centuries have undoubtedly done so. The Fathers must bear their share of the blame but not the full responsibility for those who came after them. Moreover there is much of rich and positive value that could not have been there without that risk. Like the utterances of a prophet, you can only remove the dangers from sacramental language and render it safe at the cost of removing its great evocative power for good also.

Chapter Six

THE CHURCH

THE most obvious outcome of the ministry of Jesus was the Church. However little the disciples may have understood at first of what Jesus had done for them and of the nature of the work to which he had called them, they were there. Call them what you will—disciples, brethren, followers of the way—they had a corporate existence, whose being was a result of the fact of the historic Jesus and the continuing sense of his risen presence with them. With the passage of time they were bound to consider and to articulate with increasing care what they understood to be the meaning of their existence as a body, as the Church.

Scripture uses a number of different images to describe the Church. These provided valuable material for the thought of the Fathers. The Church was the body of Christ. Union with Christ and membership of the Church belonged therefore logically together. The baptism through which a man was identified with Christ in his death and resurrection was also the means of entry into the fellowship of the Church. For what else was it to be united with Christ but to be a member of his body?

The Church was also the people of God, the true Israel. When Jew and Greek alike were prepared to scoff at the idea of a "new" faith, a religious body with no roots in antiquity, the Church could reply that it was she, and not Judaism, who was the real inheritor of the promises of the Old Testament. She was the successor of Abraham and of Jacob, of that faithful remnant which from the earliest times had always been the true vehicle of the purposes of God in the world.

But as so often it was the pressure of events that gave rise to the most important developments. The Church was an institution. Like any other institution it had to be administered. This meant the taking of decisions, including controversial decisions about which there were strong differences of opinion. It was in the process of thrashing out such practical differences that the Church was forced to consider in more precise terms what she really was and what she was intended to be. We will follow out four issues of this kind, issues which, like those relating to baptismal practice, arose most strongly in the practically-minded Western church.

1. *Mixed or pure?*

"Ye are carnal" (1 Cor. 3. 3): "ye are the body of Christ" (1 Cor. 12. 27). Those two quotations from St Paul come from the same letter and are addressed to the same group of Christians. The problem that is implicit in their contrast was not peculiar to the Corinthian church. The Church was the body of the baptized, of those whose sins had been forgiven, of those who "being born of God do not commit sin" (1 John 3. 9). But in practice the baptized were not perfect, those whose sins had been forgiven sinned again, those who were apparently born of God did commit sin. Could theory and fact be reconciled? Was it possible to say of the same group of people both "ye are carnal" and "ye are the body of Christ"?

We have already seen how this conflict of theory and experience forced the Church to tackle the problem of the forgiveness of sins committed after baptism. To reach a decision on that issue was at the same time to reach a decision about the nature of the Church. To allow further opportunities of repentance to the gross sinner and to develop a penitential system for regulating the forgiveness of such sins was to decide that the Church was not a home for perfected saints but a school for struggling sinners.

This was no single decision taken at one particular moment with full awareness of all the implications of the question. The acknowledgment of the necessity of allowing post-baptismal forgiveness was a gradual thing. It was the result of a series of decisions in response to particular problems of the moment. At each stage there was criticism and protest from a puritan element within the Church. The conflict between these two approaches came to a head in the middle of the third century.

If there is one sin that might seem to put a man more completely and more permanently outside the fellowship of the Church than any other, it is the sin of apostasy. Murder and adultery were sins which the Church did not find it easy to admit might be forgiven. But at least they did not involve a deliberate going back on one's baptism and one's faith, a direct repudiation of that by which a man had become a member of the Church. In the year A.D. 250 the Church had for the first time to face a full-scale attack of persecution by the Roman state under the emperor Decius. It was short but extremely severe. Many Christians lapsed and abjured their faith by offering the token sacrifice to pagan gods which was required by the state. Even before the wave of persecution was over many of those who had lapsed were sorry for their fall and anxious to be reinstated in the Church. What action was to be taken? Was such a reinstatement possible? The main body of the Church answered that question in the affirmative. Certainly the man who had lapsed must not be allowed to minimise his guilt, he must fulfil whatever penance the Church imposed upon him and this might have to last throughout the remaining years of his life. But even if it were only on his death-bed that he were to be

137

readmitted, he was not necessarily shut out from the Church for ever. The Church was not made up only of the perfect. She was the ark of salvation in which were to be found beasts clean and unclean; she was the field in which the wheat and the tares were to grow together until the harvest. But that answer did not win universal approval. Novatian, a man of acknowledged learning and piety, was elected rival Bishop of Rome by those who believed any forgiveness of the lapsed, even on the strictest terms, to be wrong in principle. For him the Church was by definition holy, the spotless bride of Christ. A Church which admitted back into its ranks those who had been defiled by deliberate apostasy was a Church that had lost its holiness; it was a Church that had ceased to be the Church. The only logical outcome of such a conviction was to break away from the main body and to see that the true Church be able to continue its existence in that holiness which is essential to its being. That is what Novatian did, and the Novatianist sect lived on for two centuries or more.

The same issue arose again in North Africa as a result of the great persecution under Diocletian, which marked the last years of the Church's life before her emergence into the peace of Constantine in the early years of the fourth century. On this occasion it gave rise to the Donatist schism. Many other factors, social, political and national, contributed to the rise and continuance of the Donatist church in North Africa, but its theological basis was the same as that of the Novatianist schism. It alone, it claimed, had maintained that holiness which is essential to the very being of the Church. Not only those who had formally apostatised but any who had handed over copies of the sacred Scriptures to the civil authorities in the course of the persecution were unholy and therefore automatically outside the holy Church; so also were any who remained in fellowship and communion with them. When Augustine became Bishop of Hippo in A.D. 396, Christianity in North Africa existed in two rival forms. Even in the small town of Hippo there was a rival Donatist bishop and congregation. One of Augustine's main tasks was to clarify the Catholic conception of the Church in contrast to the clear-cut puritan teaching of the Donatists.

In the first place Augustine insists that the most distinctive mark of the Church is not holiness but love. The perfectionist may claim to be preserving holiness by separating himself from those who have failed in Christian living. But that act of separation, says Augustine, does not really preserve his holiness; it only reveals his lack of love.

Nevertheless Augustine was not wholly unmoved by the Donatist line of argument. There is after all a difficulty in saying as strongly as Augustine wanted to say that the Church is at the same time the body of Christ and a place where the wheat and the tares grow together. The early Roman prophet, Hermas, describes how there appeared to him in the course of his visions an old lady representing the Church. At one point her age is explained as a symbol of her high dignity, for she is older than the rest of the creation and the very purpose of God's creative work; at another point it is a symbol of her weakness, the result of the sins of her members. Must one simply remain content with imagery of this conflicting kind? Augustine tried in two ways to show how these two firm convictions about the nature of the Church could coexist. The Donatists could not be right in their belief that the holy can be separated off as the true Church here and now. Even if the Church were to exclude all known and open sinners, she could never in the same way exclude those secret sinners whose sin is in the heart and known only to God. Holiness was a mark of the Church, but it belonged to the goal of the Church rather than to her present existence. It was only in the last day that the sheep would be separated from the goats and the wheat from the tares; only at the end of time would she be the spotless bride of Christ, perfectly prepared and adorned for her husband.

But Augustine sometimes makes what is essentially the same point in a significantly different way. He himself had come to Christianity by way of Neoplatonism. It was natural to him therefore to think not only in biblical and historical terms of the Church's goal, but to think also in Platonist terms of the true Church as already existing in the eternal realm. Under the influence of this approach Augustine sometimes speaks of the essential Church as including only those members of the visible Church who are really filled with the spirit of love. There is, therefore, as the Donatists claimed, a Church that is truly holy, but it is not the whole of the visible Church; it is an inner invisible core, whose membership is known only to God.

Neither of these lines of argument was felt by Augustine to detract from the vital importance of the visible, institutional Church. The wheat that would constitute the Church of the last day would be wheat taken out of the field of the visible Church, the true Church already in existence was an inner core of the institutional Church. As with baptism, so also membership of the visible Church was not by itself enough; but it was still essential.

2. *The Ministry*

The Church was not a home for saints but a school for sinners. Perhaps even a home for saints would need its leaders for guidance and for teaching. But a school certainly needs schoolmasters; and a school for sinners needs schoolmasters with an accredited authority which cannot easily be questioned or challenged. The ministry was not concerned only with ministering the penitential system, but it was the kind of problem which we have been discussing in the last section which was particularly important in determining the pattern of the ministry's development and the growth of its authority. It is not for nothing that the gospel texts most closely associated with the beginnings of the Christian ministry are texts which speak of binding and loosing, of the forgiving and retaining of men's sins (Matt. 16. 19; 18. 18; John 20. 23).

The letters of Ignatius of Antioch are among the earliest of all the writings of the Fathers. In them there is to be found a far greater stress on the importance and authority of the ministry, and of the bishop in particular, than in any of the writings of the New Testament, even those which stand quite close to them in date. Ignatius was disturbed about the disruptive effect which Gnostic speculations might have on the congregations of Asia Minor. To meet that threat each local congregation must remain a united and coherent group. That unity and cohesion was to be secured by absolute loyalty to its ministry, its bishop, presbyters and deacons. To act in any Church matter without the knowledge of the bishop was to render service to the devil. The bishop is the vital symbol of unity. He presides after the likeness of God and the presbyters after the likeness of the council of the apostles. No further explanation of their authority is attempted. No argument from succession or reasoning of that kind is given in support of the great respect and authority that is claimed for them. The authority of the ministry, and of the bishop in particular, is simply asserted as the key to unity in the local situation.

Irenaeus in the closing years of the second century was concerned with Gnosticism not simply as a local phenomenon but as a challenge to the Church as a whole. To him the concept of succession was one of vital importance. The Gnostics claimed for their various notions the authority of a secret tradition. They claimed to have access to a tradition of such special worth that it had been handed down by the apostles not publicly but privately to the teachers of their sect. Irenaeus' answer to all such claims was to insist that the only succession that counted was the succession in the public office of the Church. It was the succession of bishops or presbyters (Irenaeus, like the New Testament writers, does not distinguish the two terms) which really went back to the apostles. It was with them and not with any esoteric group of Gnostic teachers that the truth was to be found. Their special role within the continuing stream of the Church's life was to be the accredited guardians of the true Christian tradition which had originated with the apostles.

There is good sense in Irenaeus' argument. The public tradition of the Church did not go back so precisely without alteration to the time of the apostles as he and his contemporaries believed, but it was certainly a great deal more reliable than the secret tradition of the Gnostics. Nevertheless it would be difficult to claim that public office conferred infallibility, that it provided an absolute guarantee of true teaching. Nor does Irenaeus make such a claim. He admits that there are those who hold the office of presbyter unworthily. Scripture and the traditional summaries of the faith used in public teaching provided some kind of check on the presbyter or bishop who failed in his task of being a guardian of the truth.

But what of practical decisions? Objective checks by which the soundness of the bishop's judgment could be tested are not so easy in such cases. Who was to determine if the lapsed should be reinstated, and, if so, on what conditions? Some claimed that the proper organ for such decisions was not the men of superior office but the men of the highest sanctity. But sanctity is not something that can easily be determined beyond dispute. Nor did apparent sanctity speak with a single voice. The high-principled

Novatian would countenance no readmission whatsoever; but some of those who had suffered most for their faith in the Decian persecution offered on the strength of those sufferings to give free forgiveness to all the lapsed. That way lay chaos. In such a situation Cyprian felt himself forced to assert the authority of his office in an increasingly absolute form. Christ had founded his Church upon Peter and entrusted to him the keys of the kingdom (Matt. 16. 18, 19). The bishop stands in succession to Peter, and what was true of Peter is true of him. The Church now is founded on the bishops and every act of the Church is under their control. To rebel against the judgment of the bishop is to rebel against Christ.

Cyprian lived in difficult times. Persecution raged during much of his short episcopate and the Church was fiercely divided on the difficult issues which persecution brought in its train. It was a situation in which a firm assertion of authority on the part of the Church's leader may well have been needed. But the way in which Cyprian made that assertion shows that a shift is taking place in the relation of the Church and the ministry. The bishop is no longer just the focal point within the fundamental succession of the Church's life. The succession of bishops has become a succession in its own right. It does not so much itself depend upon the succession of the Church's life; rather the succession of the Church's life appears to be made to depend upon it.

This shift in the relationship between Church and ministry was to be taken a stage further with the teaching of Augustine. Augustine was faced with Donatist congregations and Donatist clergy on his own doorstep at Hippo and throughout North Africa. He was determined to do all that lay in his power to win them back into the Catholic Church. But what was he to say of them? They were schismatics; they did not belong to the Catholic Church.

Of that fact he had no doubt. But their clergy belonged to the same succession from the apostles as did the clergy of the Catholic Church. If succession were the vital criterion of being a bishop or a priest, then Donatist bishops and priests had every right to their title. The Donatists were outside the Church, but their clergy were in the true succession; they must therefore be validly consecrated bishops and validly ordained priests. Augustine saw this admission as one that might help to win Donatist clergy back into the Catholic fold. It would be easier for them to come over if they knew that their ordained status was fully recognised by the Catholic Church. Augustine's motives in pressing the point were conciliatory and constructive. But the isolation of ministerial order as something that can exist in separation from the Church is a division that has been as disastrous in its consequences as it is indefensible in theology.

3. *Local and universal*

Tertullian was one who, like Irenaeus, was deeply concerned with the refutation of Gnosticism. It is natural therefore that he too, like Irenaeus, should have laid great stress on the public tradition of the Church, particularly expressed and safeguarded by those who, as bishops of the various churches, stood in direct succession to the apostolic founder of their particular see. He implies that since the apostles would not have differed from one another differences could not arise between true churches. But it was an over-optimistic assumption which history failed to substantiate.

From the earliest times the Church had always thought of itself in both local and universal terms. It is the same Ignatius who emphasises so strongly the importance of the unity of the local community gathered round its bishop in whose writings the phrase "the Catholic (or universal)

Church" first appears. There was no necessary conflict between these two ideas, but the possibility of serious tension was obviously there. What was to happen if one church should find itself in conflict over some cherished conviction with other churches? This issue was first put severely to the test in a dispute over the right date for the celebration of Easter towards the close of the second century. The practice of the churches of Asia Minor differed from the practice of the Roman church and of the majority of churches in other parts of the world also. Victor, the then bishop of Rome (c. A.D. 189–97), did his best to insist on uniformity of practice and tried to coerce the Asiatic churches into acceptance of his view. But they insisted that it was more important to remain true to the local tradition which they had inherited from their own earliest saints, including St Philip and St John. Loyalty to local tradition was in their eyes a more important principle than conformity with the contemporary practice of other churches, even the church of Rome.

In the ensuing years the primary form in which this conflict between the judgment of the local church and the verdict of the wider Church found expression was the question of the authority of the church of Rome. The Roman church had always been accorded a position of special honour. Not only its location at the capital of the empire but also its close association with the two greatest of the New Testament saints, St Peter and St Paul, contributed to the special respect in which it had always been held. But was its special position one of honour only? Or did it imply some form of authority over other churches as well?

Cyprian, like the Asiatic bishops sixty years before him, found himself in sharp disagreement with the Bishop of Rome. In his case the ground of disagreement was whether or not the baptisms of schismatic groups should be recognised. Stephen, Bishop of Rome (254–7), like his predecessor Victor, set out to impose his view on the churches of North Africa. Was he not successor to the chair of Peter, the foundation apostle, the appointed ruler of the Church? Cyprian was ready to concede to Rome a primacy of honour but nothing more. He too, as we have seen, made much of the promise to Peter. But for him the successors of Peter were all bishops equally, not just the bishops of Rome. Jesus made the promise first to the one man, Peter, but he made essentially the same promise later on to all the apostles together (John 20. 22–3). The point of making the promise originally to the one only was to demonstrate clearly that the Church is one. So too the episcopate is a single whole; but it is one in which each bishop, like each apostle of old, has a full and equal share. In practice this seems to mean that for Cyprian it was important that the bishops should seek through councils and consultation to keep in step with one another. But in the last analysis each bishop was master in his own diocese; he could not be compelled to act against his own judgment by any council or any super-bishop. The unity and authority of the Church rests in the one, authoritative bishop within each diocese.

Cyprian and Stephen both died a martyr's death out of communion with one another with the issue unresolved. Stephen's interpretation of the Petrine text was at least as plausible as Cyprian's. It never won support in the East, and it was slow in gaining ground even in the West. But Rome persisted. Leo the Great (c. A.D. 450) gave to the teaching a greater fullness and a new precision. The promise to Peter gave to him a supreme authority, and it was Peter himself who is mystically present in the occupant of the episcopal see of Rome. His authority therefore is over the whole Church, while that of the other bishops belongs only to their own dioceses. But the Bishop of

Rome's authority is not simply an authority exercised over other bishops; it is most truly to be seen as an authority exercised through them. For their authority, like that of the other apostles, comes through his, that is through Peter. Leo's view was to win its way in the Western church. But the precise relationship between those two authorities, the authority of the Pope and the authority of the college of the bishops as a whole, is an issue still being debated and worked out in our own day.

4. *Unity*

The Church was one. No fact about the Church was more obvious or more certain to the mind of the Fathers than that. Christ could have only one body, only one bride; there could be only one people of God. The field might contain wheat and tares, but there was only one field; the ark might contain clean and unclean beasts but there was only one ark. Tension, as we have seen, was experienced between the claims of the local and the universal Church; since the Church was a mixed body of imperfect people such tensions were understandable and could easily be inflamed by the evil influence of ambition, pride or jealousy. But this was no reason to question the basic fact that there was one Church—one Church throughout the world expressing itself in the common life of all Christians who gathered together as the Church of Christ in each place. It was true that there were sometimes other groups in a locality claiming for themselves the name of Christian. But they were mostly Gnostic sects, so erratic in belief and practice that it was not difficult to regard them as not being genuinely Christian at all. With St John it could be said: "They went out from us, but they were not of us; for if they had been of us, they would no doubt have continued with us" (1 John 2. 19). The main body of the Church, continuing a succession of life, of teaching and of office which (so it was believed) went right back to the apostles, was not too difficult to define. This was the Church. There was and there could be only one.

From this conviction the Fathers never wavered. But they did not all draw the same conclusions from it. The logical outcome of their beliefs is obvious enough and defined by Cyprian with great force and clarity. The Church is the one ark of salvation. To be in the ark is no automatic passport to salvation for the ark contains unclean as well as clean beasts; but to be outside the ark, outside the visible, institutional Church, is to be outside the sphere of salvation. The Church is the body of Christ; there can be no salvation except through incorporation into his body. It is to the Church that the Holy Spirit was given; there and there only can his saving and sanctifying grace be received. Whatever may be believed or said or done outside the Church is totally irrelevant to man's salvation; it can contribute nothing to that union with God through Christ which is the essence of salvation.

It is a clear and consistent position. But can it be maintained? As long as the only other bodies claiming the name of Christian were erratic Gnostic sects, it was not too difficult (even if not always wholly fair) to regard them as in principle no different from the heathen. But already by Cyprian's time that was no longer the case. Novatian, as we have seen, was wholly orthodox in belief and practice and stood for the highest standards of discipline in the realm of moral conduct. Yet he had separated himself off from the main body of the Church. Was it really possible to regard him and his followers as no different from the heathen? Cyprian was true to his logic and believed that it was. Novatian's orthodoxy and piety were of no significance whatever if he had gone outside the one ark, if he had cut himself off from the one body of Christ. He could go through the motions of baptising and of celebrating the eucharist in exactly the same manner as the Church did; but that didn't make them real baptisms or real eucharists. The sacraments were sacraments of the Church. It made nonsense to talk of sacraments existing outside the Church. Since baptism is the means of a man's incorporation into the body of Christ, of his admission into the fellowship of the Church, how could it conceivably be administered by someone who was himself cut off from that body, who was not himself a member of the Church?

Cyprian's case is a strong one; but logic is not everything. It might be possible in logic, but was it possible spiritually and pastorally to regard the orthodox and devout Novatianist as no different in principle from the heathen? The Roman church, always sensitive to practical pastoral needs, found that it could not do so. This was the issue that gave rise to the great quarrel between Cyprian and Stephen of Rome. Roman practice accepted the reality of Novatianist baptism. The Roman church did not baptise (rebaptise as they would have put it) those who had already been baptised by the Novatianists. She received them into the Church with simply a laying on of hands. In the long run it was the Roman practice which prevailed. But what were its implications? How was it to be justified? These were the questions with which Augustine had to grapple as he continued to face the same issue in his dealings with the Donatists.

With Cyprian as their authority the Donatists insisted that sacraments were only genuine if administered within the Church. For them of course this meant that they would only recognise their own Donatist baptisms. But they went further than that. They also insisted on the need for personal holiness on the part of the minister performing the rite. An unholy minister could not convey the grace of a holy sacrament. It was a natural insistence for a puritan body to make, a body which regarded present holiness as essential to the very existence of the Church. This further insistence had not been central to Cyprian's position, but there were statements in his writings which could legitimately be quoted as supporting evidence on this point also.

To this second, more particularly Donatist claim, Augustine did not find it too difficult to give an answer. Such a claim, he pointed out, would involve the admission that no man could ever be sure of the genuineness of his own baptism. For if its genuineness were dependent on the personal worthiness of the officiant, who could tell whether, whatever the outward appearance, he might not have been a secret sinner all the time? The personal worthiness of the minister had to be irrelevant or the whole sacramental system would collapse. Moreover, was it not wrong to speak as if it were the individual officiant who was the conveyer of the sacramental grace? The sacraments are God's sacraments and not the minister's. The human minister is essentially a minister, a servant, a channel whom Christ uses. His personal goodness or badness cannot affect the working of the sacrament. Its power derives wholly from Christ whose sacrament it is.

But all that does nothing to meet the more fundamental question: can there be sacraments outside the Church? Augustine never deserts the basic position which was common to all the Fathers, namely that there is and can be only one body of Christ, the visible Church, and that outside that body there can be no salvation. Yet he did recognise Donatist baptisms as real baptisms, so that Donatists coming over to the Catholic Church did not need to be baptised again. How could those two convictions be combined?

Augustine meets the difficulty by drawing a distinction between the validity and the efficacy, the actuality and the benefit of a sacrament. The baptised schismatic has the gift of baptism and he cannot therefore be baptised again; but he has the gift only in a latent form and it does not profit him unless and until he comes into the fold of the Catholic Church. The schismatic by definition lacks charity, and without charity, as St Paul taught, no gift is of any profit to the man who has it. The schismatic's baptism is valid and must not be repeated; but it is not spiritually efficacious, it does not convey the saving gift that it is intended to convey unless and until its recipient joins the Catholic Church, the one body of Christ.

"I believe one, holy, catholic and apostolic Church." The four issues which we have been considering show the Western church being forced by practical needs to grapple with what is really meant by these four famous marks of the Church. The underlying difficulty is the same as that which bedevils every attempt to explore the nature of the sacraments. Can the essential meaning which the Christian sees in the sacraments be made to correspond precisely with the institutional reality? Are the essential marks of the Church always to be found in the visible institution? In the case of holiness the answer was patently No. Puritan groups made the attempt then as they do now. But the result is doubly disastrous. Augustine claimed that the spirit of separation was a denial of the spirit of love. Moreover, the need to assess achievement or failure in holiness leads to a concentration on outward, superficial things which can more easily be assessed. The holy are in danger of being identified too simply with those who have not handed over the Scriptures in time of persecution, with those who do not drink alcohol, do not gamble or whatever the outstanding shibboleth of the day may be. If the Catholic Church was sometimes lax or complacent by comparison, that is a danger to be admitted and to be guarded against. But the verdict of the Fathers was wholly right. Holiness is a mark of the Church; it is an essential part of her calling and her goal; but she is not fully holy here and now.

What then of unity? This the Fathers did believe was a clear mark of the Church's present existence. Augustine does speak of schism as rending the seamless robe of Christ. The fact of schism is a source of sorrow and distress to the Church. But it is not a rending of the Church. Schism is not something that takes place within the Church. In the desire to allow some recognition to schismatic bodies ministry and sacrament may be torn from their natural setting in the life of the Church; schismatics may have valid orders and valid sacraments, but they are still emphatically in no sense within the Church. Is this not a point at which we have to move beyond the thought of the Fathers? Does not experience teach us that, as with holiness, so unity also is something which belongs to the calling and to the goal of the Church, but that it is not always a mark of her existence here and now?

What then of apostolicity and catholicity? The continuity of the Church in time and her universality throughout the world are marks which the Fathers did well to stress against all ephemeral or purely local aberrations from the truth. But the Church's apostolicity came to be viewed in increasingly narrow terms. Episcopal succession came to be seen not as a focus of the fundamental succession of the whole life of the Church, but rather as a continuous succession in its own right. Conceived in such terms it defeated its own object, for it could actually continue outside the Church altogether. The Church's catholicity also tended in the long run to be seen in one particular form—acceptance of the supremacy of the Roman church. The acknowledgment of a single head of the whole Church by Christians from every corner of the globe would be a most impressive way of demonstrating the universality of the Church. It is not therefore necessarily the right way. Apostolicity and catholicity are essential marks of the Church. But they ought not to be treated as the kind of mark whose presence can be directly proved or guaranteed.

Church and State

The issues with which we have been concerned so far are ones which arose out of the problems of the Church's own internal life—the determination of who should be admitted into membership, of what was to be done when men failed to live up to the standards expected of them, and of who should exercise authority in such matters, disputes between churches in different places or between rival churches in the same place. But the Church did not live in a private world of her own. She was set within the Roman empire, an empire at first hostile, later tolerant and finally active in support of her interests. There was a continually changing scene in which the Church had to work out her relationship to the authority of the state.

Even while the Empire was actively involved in the persecution of the Church, the Fathers still believed that the authority of the state was God-given and designed to keep in check the injustice which would be perpetrated by the sin of men were it not for the restraining power of the civil arm. The Christian was bound therefore to respect the Emperor, to pray for him and to obey him— provided always that the obedience which was demanded of him was not one, like sacrificing to pagan gods, which clashed with his higher allegiance to the laws of God.

If Christians could think, speak and act in such a way towards the authority even of a pagan, persecuting state, a Christian Emperor was sure to be the recipient of almost unbounded reverence and honour. The tradition of ascribing divine honours to a kingly ruler was of long standing in the ancient world. The Roman Emperors had made good use of that tradition. They had given to their office a divine status which enabled it to serve as a symbol of loyalty and union throughout their scattered empire. Christians could never ascribe that kind of status to the Emperor; but they were not unaffected by the tradition. Many of the leaders of the Eastern church were ready to acclaim Constantine as an image of the Logos himself. As the Church was commissioned to fulfil the teaching role of Christ, so the Empire under a Christian Emperor was to carry out Christ's kingly office. The Christian Emperor was a fitting symbol of the monarchical ruler of heaven, by whom and on whose behalf he had been entrusted with the monarchical rule of earth.

Such sentiments were more than just the time-serving utterances of ecclesiastical politicians. In part at least they grew out of an understanding of the Emperor's role which, however mistaken, was sincerely Christian in intention and which can be traced back into the age of persecution itself. But the dangers are obvious. The actions of Constantine, let alone of later Emperors with less genuine concern for the well-being of the Church, did not always mirror the monarchical rule of heaven. The Church needed to assert for herself a greater measure of independence over against the Emperor, if she were not to be turned into the tame instrument of imperial policy.

In the closing years of the fourth century it fell to the lot of Ambrose of Milan not only to assert but effectively to practise such greater independence. At times Ambrose speaks as if there were two clearly distinguishable spheres: "Render to Caesar the things that are Caesar's and to God the things that are God's (Matt. 22. 21). Palaces belong to the Emperor; Churches to the Bishop." But this does not represent the deepest level of his thought. He did not really believe that there were two clearly separable spheres of existence, which could be kept wholly distinct from one another—any more than Jesus, when he first spoke the words which Ambrose quotes, had intended to imply that there were things of Caesar's which fall outside the sphere of God's concern.

State and Church each had their particular responsibilities; but those responsibilities did not exist in isolation, they included responsibilities in relation to each other. The Empire, for Ambrose, was not religiously neutral like a modern secular state. Religion in the ancient world was always a national as well as an individual thing. To this tradition the Old Testament added further support. Empires as well as individuals had a place in the purposes of God and must be administered in the light of that purpose. The Emperor was a Christian, a son of the Church, and must never forget that fact even in the performance of his official duties. But the state was not identical with the Church. It was not the state's task to say what decisions should be reached in matters of doctrine or of discipline, but it was her task to see that the Church had the opportunity of reaching such decisions in Church Councils and that once made they were properly enforced. It was not the state's task to persecute the heretic or impose Christian conformity by law, but it was her task to see that no official recognition was given to non-Christian public worship. Conversely it was not the Church's task to tell the state in detail how its work should be done, but it was her role to act as guardian of the state's conscience. Ambrose saw himself as Nathan to the Emperor's David. And if the Emperor were not as quick as David to admit his guilt and amend his ways, then the Church had the right, indeed the duty, to apply spiritual sanctions against him as a child of the Church in order to enforce the words of her counsel or rebuke.

If the attitude of the Eastern bishops to Constantine was liable to give rise to the sins of weakness and subservience —and did in fact do so, the attitude of Ambrose carried with it the converse danger of the sins of strength and of power. If the Church were to act as the conscience of the Emperor not only in word but with authority, could she be trusted herself to use that power and authority aright? On one occasion Ambrose required the Emperor to countermand an order for the massacre of 7,000 Thessalonians which he had given in revenge for their rioting against the local garrison; and when the cancellation arrived too late to be effective Ambrose required him to do penance for the butchery. On another occasion when an unruly horde of monks had burnt down a Jewish synagogue at Callinicum on the Euphrates, Ambrose forbade the Emperor to require a Christian bishop to be responsible for the rebuilding of a non-Christian place of worship. To Ambrose they appeared as parallel applications of the same principle; to us there appears to be a profound difference between the two cases.

Similarly once the principle of the state's support and encouragement of the Church had been accepted, it was not easy to define the point at which that support should stop. Augustine, the convert and admirer of Ambrose, shared at first the same conviction that coercion of the heretic was no part of the state's task. A true conversion had to come from the heart and not by imposition of external authority. But the Donatism with which Augustine was faced was more than just an alternative faith. It was a social and nationalist phenomenon as well as a purely religious one. Its more extreme adherents were not averse to using violence and intimidation to hold men back from going over to the Catholic Church. In this complex situation, in which heresy and lawless violence were closely tied up together, there may perhaps have been some valid arguments in favour of the suppression of Donatism by the state. What however is quite certain is that the theological argument which Augustine used was totally invalid. In applying to the situation the words of the parable, "Compel them to come in" (Luke 14. 23), Augustine had set a disastrous precedent for subsequent generations to follow.

Augustine's influence on the thought of later ages was not restricted to this particular decision about the suppression of Donatism. It was exercised at a more fundamental level by one of the great books of the age of the Fathers, *The City of God*. The book is not directly a book about Church and state, and much of its immense influence on the middle ages is based on a misunderstanding of its real nature. The sack of Rome in A.D. 410 had a psychological effect on the Roman world far in excess of its immediate military significance. Rome, for so long the centre of the ancient world, had but recently deserted her ancestral gods and turned to the God of the Christians. Was her destruction, men asked, the outcome of her change in religious allegiance?

Against the background of this question Augustine sought to write reflectively about the relation of human history and the purposes of God. The two cities about which he writes, the earthly city and the city of God, are not simply state and Church under other names. They are two principles rather than two organised societies. The earthly city is the embodiment of the principle of self-love to the point of contempt of God; the city of God is the embodiment of the principle of the love of God to the point of contempt of self. The two principles are not precisely embodied in the two institutions of state and Church.

We have already seen how in Augustine's thought, important though the visible Church is, the true Church does not correspond exactly with it. Still more emphatically the opposing, evil principle is not to be identified with the state. The danger is always there in the life of the state, the danger of domination over others for the aggrandisement of self; there are times when it has been manifested historically in the tyranny of Assyria or the imperialism of Rome. But the state does have a divinely ordained role. Its purpose is the maintenance of order, and in a fallen world that cannot be done without the use of force and of coercion. This maintenance of terrestrial peace is a necessary, though limited, purpose; the Church could not do without it and individual Christians must therefore be prepared to play their part within it. But the Church's goal belongs to a different order; it belongs to the eternal realm. The goal of the Church is heavenly peace; it is a goal which takes in but transcends the limited goal of the state.

In the last analysis the real theme of the book is not the institutions of Church and state, but the principles of love of God and love of self. It is with these ultimate realities that Augustine is primarily concerned. And it is in that fact that the book's abiding value lies. A book which was directly concerned with the terms of a concordat between the fifth-century Church and the fifth-century Empire would have little direct relevance to our present problems. A book which makes us reflect on the underlying purposes of Church and state in the light of the eternal purposes of God cannot fail to have a lasting relevance. Treated as if it were a book of the former kind the middle ages read out of it the medieval papacy. Treated as the book it really is no clear or single picture of the relation of Church and state emerges. Nor should the ideas that do emerge be treated as infallible guidance for later generations of

Christians. But in no other way could the insights of the early Church, who first grappled with this problem, be more helpfully made available for our use as we continue to grapple with the same problem in our very different situation today.

Chapter Seven

ETHICS

THEOLOGY more than ethics: theory more than practice. That is the traditional picture, the traditional indictment of the priorities of the Fathers. But is it true? It is certainly true that they were concerned about the intellectual formulation of theological truth with a passion which we find it hard to share. But the reasons that lay behind that concern were, as we have seen, not purely intellectual; they were practical and religious. The greatest thinkers were also the great preachers and pastors. Origen preached almost every day in the church at Caesarea; Athanasius and Augustine were the most indefatigable pastors of their flocks. An unbalanced picture of the life and thought of the Fathers may in part be due to the preoccupation of later generations (including this book) with the more strictly doctrinal aspect of their work. They had a strong practical and pastoral concern and were therefore fully involved in questions of conduct. These were not for them something to be contrasted with theology; they were rather a necessary and indispensable part of it.

In the realm of ethics practice is the heart of the matter. The Christian apologist did not normally claim any particular superiority for Christian ethical theory. He did claim that the difference made by Christianity could be seen in the kind of lives actually being led by ordinary Christians. Greek philosophy had been like the doctor who restricts his practice to a fashionable élite and leaves the slums uncared for. The distinctive character of Christianity was to be seen in the fact of "the simplest of Christians living lives more moderate and more pure than many philosophers". And it was this fact rather than their theoretical ideas about ethics—indeed it would be more accurate to say it was this fact in spite of what appeared to be a total lack of theoretical ideas about ethics—which first impressed their cultured contemporaries. One pagan philosopher, writing about A.D. 300, declares: "In matters of ethics, Christians neglect the more difficult matters, such as the definition of moral and intellectual virtue or the discussion of moral character and affections; they busy themselves only with exhortation, giving no account of the elements in treating of the different virtues but heaping up a haphazard collection of unintelligent precepts. But the great multitude listens to them, as one can learn from experience, and increases in virtuousness, and piety is stamped on their characters, giving rise to the type of morality which this way of life engenders and leading them gradually towards the desire for the noble."

In the sphere of ethics, then, it was the achievements of early Christian practice that were of the most immediate significance. Nevertheless that is not our concern here. What was expected of the Christian in matters of conduct had to be taught. The teaching of Jesus as recorded in the gospels is largely unsystematic in character. No teacher will remain content with a purely "haphazard collection of unintelligent precepts". He is bound to correlate and order his material in some way—even if the final outcome may still seem very haphazard to someone with a more systematic or philosophical concern. The beginnings of such systematising of Christian ethical teaching are to be seen in the New Testament itself. St Matthew has arranged the teaching of Jesus in a more systematic way than St Luke, who records much of the same material. In the epistles we find lists of virtues to be pursued and vices to be shunned. The social duties of Christians as husbands or wives, parents or children, masters or slaves, are also set out in orderly fashion. When Christians undertook this kind of systematisation, largely for purposes of instructing catechumens, they did not start completely from scratch. New Testament study suggests that the early outlines of ethical instruction to be found there are probably based on already existing outlines of moral instruction, both Jewish and Greek. This process of drawing upon both Jewish and Greek sources is still more evident and still more extensive in the writings of the early Fathers.

Jewish influence: an ethic of law

The foundation of all Jewish moral teaching was the Old Testament law. That law was also a part of the Christian's Scripture. Paul, it is true, had spoken in vigorous terms of "the curse of the law" and of Christ as being "the end of the law for righteousness to every one that believeth" (Gal. 3. 13; Rom. 10. 4). But Marcion (c. A.D. 140) and some of the Gnostics had shown what dangerous results could follow if you pushed that teaching too hard. You could drive a wedge between the creator God of the Old Testament and the God who was the Father of Jesus Christ. And if you could write off the Old Testament law like that, you were well on the way to cutting loose from any kind of moral restraint whatever. Christians, now largely free of the Jewish-Gentile tensions of Paul's day, were anxious to preserve the authority and the substance of the law's moral teaching. So there grew up, particularly in the West, the conviction that when Paul talked about Christ being the end of the law he had never meant to refer to the moral law at all. It was the ceremonial law only, the ritual enactments, which were done away by Christ and no longer had any authority over Christian practice. The moral law remained unaffected. It was fully binding upon Christians and was a firm basis for Christian moral instruction.

Thus it was natural for the early Church to approach questions of ethics in terms of law, in terms of particular injunctions understood as embodying the divine will for human life. Nor was Jewish influence restricted to the Old Testament law. Contemporary Jewish instruction was often given in the form of a description of the "two ways"; this listed the things that must be done to follow the way of life and the things that must be shunned to escape the way of death. This same outline form is borrowed and adapted for Christian use in more than one early Christian document.

Even when the aim of the teaching was to differentiate Christian practice clearly from that of Judaism, the way in which it was done was often such that the underlying similarity of spirit was really more emphasised than the intended difference of practice. Christians should fast, says one very early manual of instruction, on the fourth and sixth days of the week, and not like the hypocrites on the second and fifth. Even self-conscious opposition to Judaism could contribute to shaping the Church's moral teaching in the form of a series of prescriptive rules.

It was not unnatural to see the teaching of Jesus himself in a similar light. When St Matthew collected the teaching of Jesus together into what we call "the Sermon on the Mount", he almost certainly intended his readers to understand it as a Christian parallel to the law first given on Mount Sinai. That in any case was how the Fathers understood him. In Tertullian's eyes not only was the moral law of the Old Testament still in force; it had even been supplemented. To the law against adultery had been added a law against lust; to the law against murder had been added a law against anger (Matt. 5. 27–8; 21–2).

Did a new law mean also a new legalism? Was the freedom for which Paul had fought so hard simply lost? Did the second-century Church inherit the spirit of the Pharisee

163

and of the Judaism against which Jesus and Paul had rebelled so violently? Every historical movement loses something of its first freshness in its second and third generation. In the process of ensuring its continuation in history it has to make rules, and an element of formalism creeps in. This certainly happened in the case of the early Church. The writings of the second century do reveal a formalism and a tendency to legalism which are absent from the pages of the New Testament. That this should have happened in some measure was inevitable. What is important is to assess its extent and its real character.

The gospel was a gospel of free forgiveness offered to the sinner without regard for his merits or moral achievements. That gospel remained. It was expressed supremely in baptism. But what of life after baptism? Here, as we have seen, the Church was faced with acute problems in determining what was to be required of Christians and in regulating what was to be done when those requirements were broken. It was here that the writ of the "new law" ran.

"Oh how I love thy law," sang the psalmist (Ps. 119. 97). To the devout Jew the law was God's gracious gift to his people after redeeming them from Egypt, given for the guidance of their life within the covenant. So at its best was the "new law" to the Christian. Christ, having redeemed the new Israel through the saving waters of baptism, had given them a new law to guide them on their spiritual pilgrimage to full fellowship with God. Theodore of Mopsuestia feels the need to justify the existence of a law to direct the life of the New Israel. Strictly the life of the new age should be ordered by love alone and not by law at all. But though the Christian has been translated into the new age at his baptism, he does not yet belong wholly to it; until his actual resurrection after death he is a child of two ages, a child not only of the new age but also of the age of mortality. For that reason the basic requirement of love still needs to be broken up for man's guidance into a series of specific injunctions. This is the status of that law which Christ has graciously bestowed and by which the Christian's life must be ruled.

But, as with Judaism, so with Christianity the law did not always appear so positively and creatively as a gift for which to thank God; it appeared also in a more threatening guise. Baptism embodied God's free gift of salvation which could not be earned by any keeping of the moral law. But once received that gift had to be preserved. And the requirement for its preservation was the keeping of God's law. Thus the keeping of the law was not required to win salvation; indeed it could not do so. But it was required if a man were not to lose that salvation once given. It is here that the note of legalism creeps into early Christian teaching. Moreover when men fell short in this required keeping of the law, moral actions going beyond what the law required could play their part in making reparation for past failures. "Charity shall cover the multitude of sins" (1 Pet. 4. 8) was interpreted to mean that generous almsgiving would compensate for the sins of the giver. Not everything that Paul had fought for was lost in the teaching about Christian ethics as a "new law". But in this particular aspect of its development, much was.

Greek influence

Jewish influence on early Christian ethics was a mixed blessing. It provided a firm foundation of moral teaching whose importance is vividly illustrated by the ease with which many of the Gnostics could combine lofty religious sentiments with gross moral licence; but it also provided the Church with a strong bias towards legalistic thinking in ethics. But whatever its fruits, at least in itself it is no matter for surprise. Christianity had sprung out of Judaism. They shared the same Scriptures. Important points of affinity in

165

ethical teaching were only to be expected. But Jewish influence did not stand alone. The influence of Greek ethics was of the same level of importance.

The Christian apologist's primary argument in the sphere of ethics was, as we have seen, the greater effectiveness of Christianity in bringing ordinary people to embrace the good life. He had no desire to rebut the charge that the Church's "ethical teaching contained nothing that is impressive or new in comparison with that of other philosophers". Nor did the apologist find such similarities in ethical teaching hard to explain. Sometimes they are ascribed to the Greek teachers having borrowed their ideas from Moses, who lived well before their time. More often they are explained in terms of natural law, that "law written in men's hearts" (Rom. 2. 15), which God had implanted in man by his creation and which, though partially obscured by sin, was not totally obliterated by it. This was more than apologetic device, more than an empty compliment to the Greek ethical tradition given in the hope of securing a sympathetic audience and then safely ignored in practice. Early Christian writers did in fact draw extensively on that Greek tradition.

The extent of that borrowing can best be illustrated from two of the works of the Fathers which are most directly ethical in content. The *Sentences of Sextus* is a work consisting of 451 moral maxims, dating from about the end of the second century. Two Christian writers at the beginning of the fifth century, Jerome and Rufinus, were unable to agree whether it was the work of a pagan Pythagorean philosopher or of the martyr Bishop of Rome, Xystus II (A.D. 258). It appears in fact to be the christianisation of an already existing set of Pythagorean maxims, but it is a christianisation so slight in extent that, as Jerome points out, it contains no mention of prophets, patriarchs, apostles or even Christ himself. The *Sentences of Sextus* is an early

166

work of Christian ethics; but it is no hellenisation of the moral teaching of the Bible; it is a selection of Pythagorean teaching adapted with only very minor revision for Christian use. The other work is the first systematic Christian treatise on ethics, *On the Duties of the Clergy* (*De Officiis*) by Ambrose. It is consciously modelled on a work by Cicero of the same name, even embodying parts of Cicero's treatise in detail. Certainly the Stoic teaching of Cicero is far more extensively modified than the teaching of the Pythagoreans in the *Sentence of Sextus*, but the framework of thought in which the work is cast remains clearly Stoic. Ambrose employs the old classification of the four cardinal virtues, present in Stoicism but going back to Socrates, namely Prudence, Justice, Courage and Temperance. It is hardly the most natural classification for discussing the moral teaching of the Bible or of Christ. Such an arrangement is an indication that Roman Stoicism was more than just an interpretative medium of biblical ethics. It was an important contributory source of Christian ethics in its own right.

This assimilation of Christian moral teaching to the best of the Greek tradition of moral thought is so considerable that one has to look with some care to see the main points of difference between them. Two main differences do stand out. In the first place those Christian writers who are most ready to confess the similarity of content between Christian and Greek moral teaching also point to the new motivation which Christian teaching introduces into the situation. This was seen as the secret of its greater effectiveness in human life. This new motivation within which Christian moral teaching was set takes various forms which differ markedly in their appeal to the modern mind. On the one hand the clear Christian teaching about judgment and the life after death was used to sharpen the challenge of the moral demands of God. The fires of hell can help to keep even the martyr steadfast, for they are far greater than any earthly fire he might have to face. But even those fires, real though they be, are a lesser thing than exclusion from the divine presence which is the real essence of damnation. But the distinctively Christian motivation can take also the more attractive form of seeing moral demand as response to the sacrificial love of God in Christ. The great preacher, John Chrysostom, was one who laid great stress on the fear of hell in preaching to his recalcitrant congregation. But it is not his only ground of appeal. Preaching on the text, "Ye are not your own; ye are bought with a price" (1 Cor. 6. 20), he points out that the first half of his text, with its important moral implications, is something which is common to Christians and Greeks alike. But the second half of the text, the grounding of the moral claim in the fact of Christ's redemptive sacrifice, is a distinctively Christian insight.

Secondly the content of the teaching is not absolutely identical with that of the Greek tradition. It may be the similarity between the two which is most striking, but there is in Christian moral teaching a greater stress on the outgoing, sacrificial virtues. Hospitality, almsgiving, humility —these were not new virtues, but they figure with a new prominence in Christian teaching. (In the case of hospitality the greater prominence would be even more striking if our standard of comparison were contemporary Christian teaching.) In the teaching of the New Testament all these have their roots in the generosity of God's self-giving in Christ. It is that which gives them their special place as practical embodiments of the Christian way of love. All this continues in the teaching of the Fathers as an important emphasis in their moral teaching. But inevitably a note of caution has crept in also. Scripture commends hospitality to strangers with the reminder that "thereby some have entertained angels unawares" (Heb. 13. 2); an early Christian manual commends hospitality to travelling prophets but with the warning that, if a prophet stays for more than

168

two days or asks for money, he must be a false prophet. Scripture commends the uncalculating generosity of the widow's mite (Luke 21. 1–4); more than one early Christian manual stresses thought and care about the direction of one's giving with the aid of a quotation from an unknown source: "Let thine alms sweat into thine hand, until thou shalt have learnt to whom to give." The kind of instruction that was given was concerned not merely to describe in evocative terms the quality of moral action required of the Christian but to define in some detail the ways in which that moral teaching could be applied in practice.

Asceticism

Hospitality, almsgiving and other virtues of that kind cannot be practised without a genuine measure of self-denial. The New Testament therefore in its call to a way of self-giving love sounds also a call to self-denial, at times to self-denial of a strongly ascetic kind. Now similar ascetic denial may also be counselled for a very different kind of reason. The Gnostics taught that the natural order was essentially evil. Some deduced from that fact that it had no relevance to the life of the spirit, which was the only thing that counted. What a man did therefore with his body was a matter of indifference; the life of the spirit would be unaffected even by the grossest sensuality. But the more serious Gnostics drew a very different conclusion. If matter be intrinsically evil, the less man has to do with it the better. Fasting and celibacy in particular were taught to be of vital importance in themselves for man's escape from the world of matter and progress in the realm of the spirit. Orthodox Christians explicitly disavowed this Gnostic basis for ascetic practice. But that did not prevent something of the Gnostic spirit entering into their own teaching on the subject of asceticism.

The Christian drew his image of God as without body,

parts or passions very largely from Platonic sources. We have seen how much of the doctrinal struggles of the early centuries can best be understood as the hopeless task of trying to combine this conception of God with the biblical idea of him as self-giving love to the point of incarnation and crucifixion. Precisely the same problem affected early Christian ethics. If God be without passions and the goal of Christian living be divinisation, god-likeness, then the Christian's goal must be freedom from all passion, freedom from desire. But this goal had somehow to be combined with the idea of a practical, Christ-like love of neighbour.

These two ideals stand clearly side by side in the teaching of Clement of Alexandria. On the one hand the goal of Christian perfection is described as the eradication of all earthly passions so that freed from their encumbrance a man may concentrate wholly on the vision and the love of God. On the other hand the man who has progressed in the spiritual life is not to cut himself off in a private world of his own; he is to practise a true love of neighbour, being always ready to meet the physical and spiritual needs of his less mature brethren. In Clement these ideals co-exist. But once let love of God and love of neighbour be felt to pull in different directions in this way and there is no doubt which must win in a genuinely religious tradition. If progress in the vision of God is directly proportionate to the measure of a man's withdrawal from the things of the world, then the genuinely religious man has no option but to adopt the life of the solitary hermit. So there grew up the ideal of ascetic piety in which man seeks the eradication of the passions, seeks consciously to rid himself as far as possible of all that is naturally and distinctively human.

At its best this ideal represents a wholehearted desire to know God above all else and at all costs, before which one can only stand ashamed. At its worst it reveals a harsh unnatural hatred of God's gifts which is intolerable even to contemplate—Jerome telling husband, wife or mother to rejoice at the death of partner or child, not because the one who has died has gone "to be with Christ which is far better", but because they themselves have been set free by their bereavement from something which was previously a distraction from the highest service of God. Yet even at its best it is open to serious criticism. Its underlying conviction that God is most fully to be known by escape from the phenomenal world rather than through the sacramental use of it is Greek rather than biblical in origin. Moreover, where that full knowledge of God is believed to require a detachment not only from material things but also from people, it gives rise to a subtle form of self-centredness. The man whose sole concern is to lose himself in God may seem to have reached the highest pinnacle of spirituality, but he may in fact be guilty of a too exclusive concern with self. This danger was fully recognised by those who in the fourth century initiated and guided the development of the monastic system. They stressed the importance of belonging to a monastic community, and often also of practical service to the wider community outside, as an antidote to the self-concern which could so easily be engendered in those who aspired to the purely solitary life.

Life in the world

The growth of monasticism had many causes. One at least was the Church's failure to find an answer to the question of how to live a convincingly Christian life in society. This problem became most acute in the years after Constantine, when the Church was no longer a persecuted minority but included many people in positions of responsibility for ordering the life of society. But the problem, if less acute in earlier centuries, had always been there. The calling of the Church was to a life that was in the world but not of it. "What the soul is in the body, that Christians are

171

in the world", as one early writer puts it. "We are not Brahmins or naked holy men of India," says Tertullian in his Apology addressed to the Roman world, "who exile themselves from ordinary human life. We live among you, we eat the same food, we wear the same clothes, we have the same habits, we are under the same necessities of existence. We make use of the forum and the market, the baths and the shops and all the other social institutions of ordinary life. We sail and fight alongside you; we farm and trade alongside you." The Christian's aim was to live his life alongside his non-Christian fellow-citizens but to show that it could be lived with a new quality, with a new spirit. But this ideal was not easily achieved. Social life was so closely interwoven with rites of pagan worship that the Christian often felt himself to have no option but to withdraw from social intercourse and social responsibility, with the result that in the eyes of Tacitus the most obvious characteristic of Christian behaviour was hatred of the human race.

The moral dilemma which faced the Christian in society is well illustrated by the problem of the legitimacy of taking human life. The teaching of Jesus was held to rule out such an action absolutely for the Christian. It was out of the question for those who had been taught to love their enemies and never to requite evil with evil. When the Lord told Peter to put away his sword, says Tertullian, he disarmed every soldier. It was unlawful therefore for a Christian to volunteer for the army. A man who was already a soldier before his conversion would be well advised to give up his profession if he could. If he stayed on as a soldier, he must be prepared to refuse to carry out any order to perform an execution, even if it be at the price of his own life in martyrdom. Yet at the same time the Church, as we have seen, regarded the authority of the state, based on force, as something to be accepted, not only because such acceptance was inevitable but because that authority was a God-given authority to control the ravages of sin in the world. The civil power "beareth not the sword in vain: for he is the minister of God, a revenger to execute wrath upon him that doeth evil" (Rom. 13. 4). The exercise of the sword was regarded as a God-given role, but one which no Christian would ever be justified in performing. Intellectually it was an intolerable position; but practically it was possible as long as Christians were a persecuted minority. An attempt to justify it was made by claiming that Christians did their share of fighting for the Emperor by prayers of intercession. Was it not reasonable that, like pagan priests, they should be exempt from activities that might lead to the staining of their hands with the shedding of human blood? But in the Constantinian age such a position was no longer tenable. As Augustine saw with particular clarity, if the state has a function to fulfil which God wills to be fulfilled, then it must be right for Christians to participate in the fulfilment of that function. And if in the fulfilment of that function in a sinful world capital punishment and war are necessary, then Christians must be prepared to participate even in them.

But the tension remained. It was no longer a question of Christians living under the protection of a civil authority exercised by pagans in a way which Christians recognised as necessary but in which they were unwilling to participate. The civil authorities were now Christian; their enforcement of authority with all that that involved was recognised as something that it was proper for Christians to do. Nevertheless it was still felt to be a far from perfect form of activity for a Christian. There was a conflict between the teaching of Jesus and the taking of a human life; yet human life had to be taken in the maintenance of law and order. A Christian might do it, but hardly a Christian who aspired to perfection. Basil of Caesarea even suggests that soldiering in a just cause is not wrong but that the man who kills in the course of it would do well to abstain from receiving communion for three years. Indeed did not the highest way of Christian life involve not only the avoidance of such compromise, but freedom from all forms of worldly distraction whatever? A man could be a soldier or a magistrate and at the same time be a Christian; he could not be a soldier or a magistrate and at the same time a Christian wholly dedicated to full growth in the knowledge of God.

Double standard

Pressures of this kind led naturally to the development of a double standard in ethical demand, a "pass" standard for those who were content with the basic requirements of Christian discipleship and an "honours" standard for those who aspired to perfection. Was this after all not implicit in the story of the rich young ruler as told by St Matthew (19. 16–22)? "If thou wilt enter into life," said Jesus, "keep the commandments . . . if thou wilt be perfect, go and sell that thou hast and give to the poor, and thou shalt have treasure in heaven." Basic Christian moral instruction was the new law, a minimum standard required of everyone who would enter into life, or, more accurately, who would preserve the life which he had received at his baptism. But a minimum is something which can be exceeded. A measure of almsgiving could be required; but the aspirant for perfection would go beyond that measure by giving away all his possessions and espousing poverty. If the unprofitable servant be the man who has done all the things that were commanded him (Luke 17. 10), then the good and faithful servant, so Origen argued with relentless logic, must be the man who has done more than was commanded him.

The call to virginity and celibacy can hardly have been expected to meet with universal response. Nor was there any need that it should, for marriage was never regarded as wrong in orthodox circles; that would have been false

Gnostic dualism. But it was regarded as a second best. Was that not what St Paul had taught in 1 Corinthians 7? Celibacy was another example of how the aspirant for perfection could go beyond what was required of him.

Thus the two standards were not just two stages, a way for the beginners in Christian discipleship and a way for those who had already travelled some distance along the Christian road. Nor were they just two different kinds of life, differing vocations for people of differing temperaments. They were different standards. There was a lower and a higher way. Life in the world was permitted; but the ascetic life was better.

The world has been enriched by much depth of spirituality, by much nobility of sacrifice in the lives of those who have turned their backs on the world to follow the ascetic path. But the concept of the two standards cannot be allowed to stand unchallenged. Its root conviction is that God is to be found pre-eminently in withdrawal from the world. The early Church firmly repudiated the dualism of the Gnostics which regarded the natural world as evil. Yet she never really accepted that God can be as fully served within the affairs of the world as in seclusion from them. The reasons for her doubts and her hesitations are obvious. But they have to be overcome. Nothing less is adequate to the faith of the incarnation. To work out in practice the implications of that conviction that life in the world can be Christian in just as full a sense as the life of monastic seclusion is the unceasing task of the Church in every age.

Augustine and Pelagius

If the moral achievement of the ordinary Christian was the legitimate boast of the second-century apologist, his moral failures were the despair of the fifth-century proponent of the Christian faith. The legislation of the Emperor Theodosius towards the end of the fourth century meant that it now required the same kind of moral courage to remain a pagan as had once been required to confess Christianity. Many of those who flocked into the Church at the close of the fourth century were content not merely with the lesser, but still exacting, demands made of the Christian living in the world; they were content with a nominal church membership in which any kind of moral demand was largely ignored. Something had gone badly wrong with the new moral incentive which Christianity had introduced into the Graeco-Roman world. It is against this background that the dispute between Augustine and Pelagius has to be seen.

Pelagius was a British monk, one who took seriously the challenge to perfection which the monastic calling symbolised. He was appalled by the laxness of moral standards which he encountered at Rome. The prayer of Augustine from the *Confessions*, "Give what thou commandest and command what thou wilt", shocked him. It seemed to him to undermine the foundation of that moral effort which was the primary need of the times. For Pelagius the essence of the moral life was the determined exercise of the human will. In natural law, in the Old Testament, in the teachings of Jesus, in baptismal forgiveness, in the initial endowment of man with free-will God had given to the Christian all the requisite conditions and assistance for moral success. Where there was gross failure the cause was obvious, it was moral slackness. And the remedy was equally obvious; it was stern moral exhortation.

Pelagius' view is the common-sense view of the ordinary man, the immediate reaction of the moral reformer. No doubt many moral failures are, in part at least, a result of moral slackness and can be cured by moral exhortation. But it is certainly not the root of man's problem. One cannot treat each individual moral act as an isolated phenomenon on its own; one has to deal in terms of a total

176

developing character. One cannot even treat each individual person as an isolated phenomenon on his own; he has to be seen in his organic relationship with others, with his predecessors by heredity and with his contemporaries by environment. Ethics cannot be divorced from psychology; one cannot say what a man should do, one certainly cannot help him to put it into practice, without a knowledge of the way in which the whole interior life of man actually functions. All this Augustine saw. The formal expression that he gave to some of his insights may at times have been seriously astray (we have seen earlier the unfortunate implications of his formulated doctrine of original sin). But the real measure of his greatness is the fact that he saw it, and that he recognised the fundamental importance of what he saw for the moral life.

The sense in which the will is free is impossible to define. Augustine always felt that he could continue to maintain the reality of that freedom in some sense. Even if a man is bound to sin, it is not a matter of some external force making him sin; man sins by his own act and with the consent of his own will. But this is not the most important issue for practical ethics. The freedom, Augustine argues, that really matters is not the theoretical freedom of choice, the freedom in accordance with which I can choose either to tell the truth or to tell a lie to my friend on any particular occasion. The freedom that really matters is the freedom to live out the truth in all circumstances, the freedom to remain true to my highest aspirations all the time without continually spoiling them through my own weakness. The secret of this kind of freedom is not moral exhortation; too direct a concentration on moral demand can be self-defeating. This freedom has to be won at the deeper level of the affections. It is a truer and stronger love of the good that is the secret of moral progress. For such love there is only one source, the God who himself is love. "The love of

177

God" (by which Augustine understands our love for God rather than God's love of us) "is shed abroad in our hearts by the Holy Spirit which is given unto us" (Rom. 5. 5). The Holy Spirit is not an external adjunct to prop up our wills, while those wills remain clear and distinct entities on their own. The Holy Spirit is the love by which we love God and our neighbour. Our love of the good is not something which we have to achieve on the basis of and with the help of our religious union with God. The two things are one. Our union with God is God's dwelling in us as love. The fundamental Christian answer to moral failure is not to call for greater moral effort but for greater openness to the love of God.

EPILOGUE

THE rich variety of its contents is a part of the glory of the Bible. But it is also a source of puzzlement, even of embarrassment, to those who seek to regulate their understanding of God and of his working in the world by what they learn from Scripture. For Scripture does not offer one, clear, consistent and unmistakable account of the nature and the ways of God. It has shown itself in the course of history to be patient of a disconcertingly large number of different readings. This problem is one which has been with the Church from the very beginning. The Fathers were the Church's leaders in the realm of thought as she grappled with it for the first time.

Subsequent generations have ascribed great weight to the answers which they gave. Rival schools of thought have vied with one another to claim the authority of the Fathers for their particular interpretation of the faith. On the shelves of my theological college library there stood a book whose title was a gross and deliberate misapplication of some words of Scripture: *Whose are the Fathers?* (Rom. 9. 5). I never got beyond the preface which claimed that the book would show how completely the Fathers supported the Anglican (as opposed to the Roman) position. Such a treatment of the Fathers is disastrous both for our reading of the past and for our living of the present. For if we believe that we can find the answers to our contemporary questions in their texts, we shall distort what they have written; and if we believe that what they have written provides the answers that we need, we shall fail to grapple with the living issues of the day.

Today there is a wide recognition that the Fathers did

not ask precisely the questions which we ask, or raise them in just the way in which we cannot help raising them, and that therefore their answers cannot be ours. Our temptation may therefore be to go to the other extreme and to ignore the Fathers altogether. But that would be to do them less than justice. They stood nearest in time to those events which are of central importance to Christian faith and they were the first to attempt to answer in coherent form the questions which are inevitably raised by those events and by the faith that has sprung from them. The answers that they gave were of course conditioned by the times in which they lived, but they were also the fruit of acute minds wedded to profound faith. Many of their insights have an abiding value as a contribution to Christian thinking in their own right. But the particular importance of their teaching for us is greatly enhanced by the fact that it has provided the ground plan for the development of theological ideas in the Church ever since; whether we recognise it or not the work of the Fathers is an important constitutive part of the background of our own thinking. To ignore them is to cut ourselves off from our heritage; it is to refuse to see the issues of the faith today in their proper historical perspective. The problems of contemporary theology are new in form, but they are not wholly new in substance. The Fathers cannot solve them for us. That task remains ours. But we limit unnecessarily the resources with which we attempt it if we believe that it can be done without reference to them.

APPENDIX

List of Fathers (and others) mentioned in the text (dates of birth are mostly not certainly known and should be regarded as only approximate).

AMBROSE OF MILAN (339–397): elected Bishop of Milan by popular acclaim when a high state official and still only a catechumen; baptised and consecrated 374; outstanding preacher; vigorous anti-Arian; writer on ethics; leading role in Church-state affairs.

APOLLINARIUS OF LAODICEA (310–390): Bishop of Laodicea in Syria from about 361; strong anti-Arian; friend of Athanasius; outstanding scholar; respected champion of orthodoxy for first sixty years of his life; condemned for his denial of Christ's human soul at Council of Constantinople, 381.

ARIUS, presbyter of Alexandria. Condemned for his teaching that the Son is not of the same "substance" as the Father at Council of Nicaea, 325; died on eve of proposed readmission to the Church, 336.

ATHANASIUS OF ALEXANDRIA (295–373): Bishop of Alexandria from 328; unwavering leader of anti-Arian cause.

AUGUSTINE OF HIPPO (354–430); child of pagan father and Christian mother; student of Neoplatonism; successful professor of rhetoric until conversion under the influence of Ambrose in Milan, 386; Bishop of Hippo in North Africa from 396; prolific author, primarily in doctrinal field.

BASIL (THE GREAT) OF CAESAREA (330–379): Bishop of Caesarea in Cappadocia from 370; leading member of the Cappadocian Fathers (together with Gregory of Nazianzus and Gregory of Nyssa); ecclesiastical statesman, able organiser and gifted scholar; leading defender of Nicene orthodoxy in his day; active role in development of monasticism and liturgy.

CLEMENT OF ALEXANDRIA: head of catechetical school of Alexandria about 200; first extensive synthesis of Christian faith and Hellenistic philosophy.

CYPRIAN OF CARTHAGE: wealthy pagan with good rhetorical training; converted to Christianity in middle age, 246; elected Bishop of Carthage, 248-9; able administrator in difficult times of persecution; author of several letters and short treatises, mainly on practical subjects; martyred 258.

CYRIL OF ALEXANDRIA: Bishop of Alexandria from 412; died 444; able scholar but unscrupulous ecclesiastic; bitter opponent of Nestorius.

CYRIL OF JERUSALEM: Bishop of Jerusalem from 348; died 386; famous for his lectures to catechumens, published from the shorthand notes of one of his hearers.

EUNOMIUS: Bishop of Cyzicus on the Hellespont for short period from 360; able leader of extreme Arians in second half of fourth century; main opponent of Cappadocian Fathers; died 394.

EUSTATHIUS OF SEBASTE: Bishop of Sebaste in Armenia from 357; originally friend of Basil of Caesarea and active proponent of monasticism; later his bitter opponent; a man of austere life; opposed to full Arianism but also to full Nicene orthodoxy.

EUTYCHES: head of a large monastery near Constantinople; a man of piety rather than scholarship; condemned in his old age at the Council of Chalcedon 451 for denying the two natures of Christ after the incarnation.

GREGORY OF NAZIANZUS (330-390): Bishop of Constantinople in 381 but resigned almost immediately; close friend of Basil of Caesarea (q.v.); poet, gifted preacher and defender of orthodoxy.

GREGORY OF NYSSA (335-394): Bishop of Nyssa in Cappadocia from 371; brother of Basil of Caesarea (q.v.); ablest of the Cappadocian Fathers as philosopher and theologian; extensive writer on doctrine and the spiritual life.

HERMAS: author of a book of visions, known as the "Shepherd" of Hermas written about 140; a freedman, reputedly brother of the Bishop of Rome of his day; a simple, earnest Christian of narrow outlook.

IGNATIUS OF ANTIOCH: the most striking personality amongst the very early Fathers; famous for seven surviving letters written when, as Bishop of Antioch in Syria, he was being taken to Rome to suffer martyrdom there about 110.

IRENAEUS OF LYONS: Bishop of Lyons in Southern France from about 177 to 202; the outstanding theologian of the second century; author of a major work in five books against the Gnostics.

JEROME (347–420): educated in Rome, a man of immense scholarship; translated the Bible from the original Hebrew and Greek into Latin; promoted the ascetic life; involved in much bitter controversy; not a creative theologian.

JOHN CHRYSOSTOM (John of the Golden Mouth): brought up in Antioch, ordained priest there in 386, where he proved a brilliant preacher and biblical expositor; unwillingly made Bishop of Constantinople in 398; fell foul of the imperial court because of his vigorous but tactless reforming zeal; deposed in 403; died in exile, 407.

JUSTIN MARTYR: converted philosopher, most famous of the second-century apologists; martyred in Rome probably in 165.

LEO THE GREAT: strong Bishop of Rome from 440–61; did much to exalt the position of the see of Rome both by his teaching and his personality.

MARCION: son of the Bishop of Sinope in Pontus; excommunicated in Rome about 144; rejected the Old Testament, distinguishing the loving Father of Jesus from the just creator of the Old Testament; has affinities with Gnostics but lacks their interest in speculation; founded Marcionite churches; strongly ascetic in practice.

NESTORIUS: monk of Antioch and renowned as a preacher; made Bishop of Constantinople in 428; unpopular for reforming zeal; deposed in 431 at the Council of Ephesus for dividing too sharply between the divine and human natures of Christ; died not earlier than 451.

NOVATIAN: a leading presbyter at Rome in mid-third century; was made rival Bishop of Rome in 251 by the supporters of a strict puritan discipline, thus creating Novatianist schism; author of an able and orthodox treatise on the Trinity.

ORIGEN (185–253): son of Christian parents; teacher in catechetical school of Alexandria, 203–230; ordained in 230, forbidden to teach in Alexandria and moved to Caesarea in Palestine for remainder of his life; the outstanding scholar of his age and a voluminous author; he excelled as apologist, preacher, biblical expositor, writer on the spiritual life, and speculative theologian; his bold speculations led to doubts about his orthodoxy during his lifetime in Alexandria and more widely after it, but his influence was still immense; many of his works are lost and many others survive only in Latin translations which are not always reliable; died in 253 as a result of torture received in persecution.

PELAGIUS: British lay monk; lived in Rome from 384 until its sack in 410; respected for his moral austerity, but teaching condemned at Rome in 418, and in the East in 431, for the inadequacy of its account of original sin and divine grace.

RUFINUS (345–410): born near Aquileia in North Italy; one-time companion, later bitter opponent of Jerome; travelled extensively in the East and translated many Greek works into Latin, especially the works of Origen.

SABELLIUS: possibly a Libyan by birth; taught in Rome in early third century and excommunicated there about 220 for his failure to distinguish between the persons of the Father and the Son.

TERTULLIAN: a lawyer of pagan origin; converted to Christianity about 195; wrote extensively in Carthage with the style of a brilliant advocate; writings include mainly apologetic, anti-heretical (especially Marcion) and practical ascetic works; about 207 he joined the puritan Montanist sect and some of his writings date from that period; died not earlier than 220.

THEODORE OF MOPSUESTIA: close friend of John Chrysostom; ordained priest in Antioch about 383; Bishop of Mopsuestia in Cilicia from 392; died in 428; outstanding scriptural exegete of the Antiochene school; later regarded as a heretical precursor of Nestorian teaching; his works have mostly survived only in Syriac translations preserved by the Nestorian churches.

THEODOTUS the leather-worker from Byzantium: taught in Rome in closing years of the second century and excommunicated by Victor, Bishop of Rome, for his denial of the divinity of Christ.

BIBLIOGRAPHY

Biographical

H. von Campenhausen: *The Fathers of the Greek Church* (A. & C. Black 1963).

H. von Campenhausen: *The Fathers of the Latin Church* (A. & C. Black 1964).

G. L. Prestige: *Fathers and Heretics* (SPCK 1948).

Doctrinal

J. N. D. Kelly: *Early Christian Doctrines* (A. & C. Black 1958).

Historical

W. H. C. Frend: *The Early Church* (Hodder & Stoughton 1965).

Reference

F. L. Cross: *The Early Christian Fathers* (Duckworth 1961).
B. Altaner: *Patrology* (Nelson 1960).

Translations

Most of the principal works of the Fathers are available in translation. An excellent selection well translated will be found in the first eight volumes of Library of Christian Classics (SCM Press 1953-6).

Vol. I: Early Christian Fathers (including Ignatius and Irenaeus).

Vol. II: Alexandrian Christianity (i.e. selections from Clement and Origen).

Vol. III: Christology of the Later Fathers (including

Athanasius "On the Incarnation" and selections from the Cappadocian Fathers).

Vol. IV: Cyril of Jerusalem.

Vol. V: Early Latin Theology (i.e. selections from Tertullian, Cyprian, Ambrose and Jerome).

Vols. VI–VIII: Augustine.

Documents in Early Christian Thought, edited by Maurice Wiles and Mark Santer (Cambridge University Press 1976), contains translated extracts from the writings of the Fathers covering the full range of subjects discussed in this book.

INDEX

Adam, 58, 71, 91–2, 96–101, 120
agape, 123–4
Alexandria, school of, 65, 77–8, 123, 127–8
almsgiving, 118, 168–9
Ambrose, 154–6, 167, 181
Antioch, school of, 65, 78–9, 123, 127
Apollinarius, 67–72, 181
Arius, 37–40, 63–7, 181
asceticism, 169–71
Athanasian creed, 52–3
Athanasius, 40–3, 66–7, 69, 83–6, 103, 160, 181
atonement, 99–103, 107–9
Augustine, 49–52, 55, 92, 97–9 105–8, 120, 129, 133, 139–40, 143–4, 150–2, 156–8, 160, 173, 175–8, 181

baptism, 87–8, 110–23, 135, 149–51
Basil, 43, 46, 173, 181

Cappadocian Fathers, 43–8, 50, 181
Chalcedon, Council of, 9, 79–82
Clement of Alexandria, 18, 23, 87, 170, 182
Constantinople, Council of, 42, 45, 72
Cyprian, 131, 143, 145–6, 148–9, 182
Cyril of Alexandria, 77–8, 94, 182
Cyril of Jerusalem, 113, 127, 131, 132, 182

divinisation, 41, 60, 91–2, 170
Donatists, 138–9, 143–4, 149–50, 156–7

Ephesus, Council of, 72, 76
eucharist, 69, 123–34
Eunomius, 45, 182
Eustathius, 45, 182
Eutyches, 79, 182

Gnostics, 88–90, 111, 130, 141–2, 165, 169, 175
Gregory of Nazianzus, 43, 71, 102, 131, 182
Gregory of Nyssa, 43, 46–7, 88, 102, 111, 113, 128, 182

Heraclitus, 25
Hermas, 118, 139, 183
Holy Spirit, 35, 44–5, 95, 114–17, 127, 178

Ignatius, 125, 141, 144–5, 183
infant baptism, 119–21
Irenaeus, 18, 27, 57–8, 71, 91–3, 100–1, 111, 126, 130, 141–2, 183

Jerome, 166, 171, 183
John Chrysostom, 132, 168, 183
Justin Martyr, 27–8, 126, 130, 183

law, Jewish, 162–5
law, natural, 166–8
laying on of hands, 114–17, 121
Leo, 146–7, 183
Logos, 15, 24–31, 61, 87–8

Marcion, 162, 183
ministry, 140–3

Nestorius, 76–7, 184
Nicaea, Council of, 41–2, 45
Novatian, 138, 148, 184

189